A feminist ethicist and psychotherapist with over twenty years experience, Betty McLellan is the author of *Help! I'm Living with a Man Boy,* which has been translated into sixteen languages. She is also the author of *Overcoming Anxiety* (1992), *Beyond Psychoppression* (1995), and *Unspeakable: A feminist ethic of speech* (2010). With a focus on both the personal and the political, Betty successfully combines her work as a psychotherapist with a broader emphasis on a feminist ethical analysis and activism. She lives in Townsville, North Queensland.

T0308120

Other books by Betty McLellan

Unspeakable: A Feminist Ethic of Speech (2010)
Help! I'm Living with a ~~Man~~ Boy (1999, 2006)
Beyond Psychoppression: A Feminist Alternative Therapy (1995)
Overcoming Anxiety (1992)

Ann Hannah, My (Un)Remarkable Grandmother

A Psychological Biography

Betty McLellan

Published in Australia by Spinifex Press, 2017

Spinifex Press Pty Ltd

PO Box 5270, North Geelong, Victoria 3215 Australia
PO Box 105, Mission Beach, Queensland 4852 Australia

www.spinifexpress.com.au
women@spinifexpress.com.au

Editors: Pauline Hopkins, Renate Klein and Susan Hawthorne
Cover design: Deb Snibson
Cover photo: held in private collection
Author photograph: Coralie McLean
Typesetting: Helen Christie, Blue Wren Books
Typeset in Adobe Gramond Pro
Printed by McPherson's Printing Group

National Library of Australia Cataloguing-in-Publication data:
McLellan, Betty, 1938– author
Ann Hannah, my (un)remarkable grandmother : a psychological biography /
Betty McLellan

9781925581287 (paperback)
9781925581317 (ebook: epub)
9781925581294 (ebook: pdf)
9781925581300 (ebook: kindle)

Includes bibliographical references.
Hannah, Ann
Grandmothers—Australia—Biography.
Women immigrants—Australia—Biography.
British—Australia—Biography.

For my siblings

Ron McLellan
Joan Ware
Beverley McEwen

Contents

Acknowledgements

Writing this book has afforded me the opportunity to look again at each member of my family of origin, and here I acknowledge and thank them for their contribution to the life I have been fortunate enough to live. If anyone had suggested twenty years ago that I write my grandmother's story, I would have been puzzled and slightly amused because, as I would have explained, there was nothing to write about. Ann Hannah Stickley was just an ordinary grandmother – a good woman, but an unremarkable woman.

I am now so grateful that my feminist consciousness prompted me to look deeper in an attempt to understand the situation of women in past generations, and that my involvement in the study of psychology led me to analysing my own grandmother. What a rich and satisfying experience it has been for me! I thank her for the positive influence she has had on my life.

I acknowledge and thank both of my parents, too, as well as my brother and two sisters for all that they have been to me over many years. I especially want to acknowledge the conversations I had with my sisters, Joan and Bev, during the writing of this book. The sharing of memories, the anecdotes, the comments and the family photos were all very helpful. Especially important to me was their encouragement to keep going with this project.

My task was made easier in the early stages of my research and writing by Bev's searching of online records. Her skill at finding and interpreting details of Nana's original family was invaluable as background to the whole book. Special thanks to my cousin Pat Prior, daughter of Annie May (Aunty May) whose story of sexual abuse is told in chapter four. Sadly, Pat died suddenly last year but I want to record my gratitude to her for her willingness to share with me some of the painful details her mother had revealed to her.

To those who shared with me their personal stories of displacement and gave permission for me to recount those stories in the book, I offer my heartfelt thanks.

To my friend Coralie McLean who read every word of every version of every chapter and gave invaluable and insightful suggestions all the way through, I say a huge thank you. Finally, to the wonderful women at Spinifex Press, in particular Renate and Susan (publishers) and Pauline (editor), thank you for your helpful comments and warm support.

Introduction

"A cup of tea fixes everything." That was Ann Hannah's remedy for all the ills of life. Whenever one of us was distressed or unhappy: "I'll make you a nice cup of tea." Whenever Mum was exhausted from dealing with the highs and lows in the lives of her four children: "I'll put the kettle on. A cup of tea will make you feel better."

Who was this woman who appeared to have such a simple solution to all of life's problems? Ann Hannah Stickley was my grandmother. By society's standards, she was an unremarkable woman who lived an unremarkable life and died an unremarkable death, and whose passing was noticed only by her immediate family. But, in a quiet unobtrusive way, her life was remarkable.

Born in nineteenth-century London, she migrated to Australia at the age of 40 with her husband and four children, and died in Brisbane at the age of 97. In my growing up, Ann Hannah was always there – in our home. There was my mother, father, older brother Ron, older sister Joan, younger sister Beverley, and me. I was the third of four siblings. Nana came to live with our family before I was born, when Ron was about six months old and so, from the moment I was born till I left home at nineteen, there was never a time when she was not part of my life.

As I understand it, after Nana was widowed, she lived by herself in the rented house she had shared with her husband before his death. Family legend has it that, when my parents were away on holidays, Mum's two sisters, May and Em, decided that their mother would be better off giving up her home and living with family members. The plan was that she would live three months at a time with each of her three daughters and their families (a recipe for instability and a sense of homelessness, if ever there was one). When Mum and Dad returned from holidays, they were told of the plan. And so it happened. Nana lived the first three months with Aunty May and the second three months with Aunty Em. Then, after three months with Mum and Dad, she was not inclined to leave because, as the story goes, my father was so much easier to get along with than her other two sons-in-law. The household was much more peaceful and she felt less like an intruder. So began the approximately 45 years of her life in my parents' home – through the births, and growing up, and leaving home as adults of my three siblings and me.

The strange thing is that, even though Ann Hannah was an integral part of my life for so long, I have always felt somewhat removed from her, as if there was very little emotional connection between us. My siblings felt the same. Whenever I thought about it over the years, I concluded that our grandmother was simply more comfortable relating on a practical level than on an emotional one. While she was never a warm and cuddly person, I must stress that she was also never cold and distant. She was always approachable and we knew that she cared for us, but she just seemed to prefer to focus on practical everyday details.

While I was never particularly bothered about not feeling an emotional connection, I have found myself in recent years wanting to delve into her past in order to know her more intimately. It is hard to explain what brought on this desire. Maybe it's that I am growing older and, like many people in my age cohort, have developed an interest in knowing more about my ancestors. Maybe it's that, as a psychotherapist, I have a professional curiosity about what makes people tick, that is, about what past experiences and inner secrets form their personality and dictate the kinds of lives they lead. Or maybe it's that I am a feminist with a particular interest in knowing about the struggles that generations of women in times past had to endure living as second-class citizens under much more serious patriarchal dominance than I have known in my own lifetime.

Whatever the explanation for my latter-day interest in delving into my grandmother's past (and I suspect that it's a combination of all three of the options just mentioned), I decided to do it and, for a time, struggled to find a way to analyse Ann Hannah's life that would both help me 'discover' more about her and, at the same time, do justice to the remarkable person that she was.

My own experience of her was that she was an incredibly industrious woman. She was always busy, always careful to 'pull her weight' in terms of housework, childcare, shopping and cooking. She had no money to speak of but was always generous with what she had. On pension day, once a fortnight, she would put on a 'going out' dress and hat (always a hat), catch a tram into the city (Brisbane) and come home laden with food for the family – sensible food like sliced ham, tomatoes, vegetables. Nothing frivolous or wasteful. Sometimes, too, she would buy children's clothes that were on sale. She loved to find a bargain and we were often the recipients of her discoveries.

I have a pleasant memory of going with my grandmother on one of her ritualistic, pension-day, visits to the city. This was a most unusual situation because she always went by herself, no doubt so that she could take her time window-shopping and browsing the shops. My going with her probably came about because I was not yet old enough to go to school, my two older siblings would have been in school, younger sister not yet born, and perhaps my mother had an appointment that she preferred to

3

go to alone. Whatever the reason, the plan was made that I would go with Nana, but I would not have gone willingly. I'm sure that I would have been very unhappy about the arrangement because I never wanted to be far away from my mother. So, as I interpret it now, Nana bribed me. She promised that she would buy me a "bloody big ice cream" from an ice cream shop in town. That obviously did it for me because I went and it turned out to be a pleasant experience.

For some time after that, the story was repeated in our extended family that, when we arrived home from the city and my mother asked me what Nana had bought for me, I said "a buddy big ice cream". Every time the story was told after that, everyone laughed and it made me feel good. I obviously didn't understand the joke but I never felt that anyone was laughing *at* me. Nana would look at me and smile as if we, together, had brought about that happy moment.

As with so many memories we have from early childhood, I have no idea if I remember the actual moment I said "a buddy big ice cream" or if the memory comes from the retelling, but the important thing is that it was a positive event that I shared with my grandmother.

Ann Hannah was the only grandparent my siblings and I ever knew. Dad's father was killed in action in France toward the end of World War I, on 29 September 1918 when my father was seven years old. His mother married again but, after my father's death, I found an official document stating that my father David Rankin McLellan was under the guardianship of his grandmother. I have no knowledge of how that came about but I do know from stories Dad told that the relationship with his grandmother was a happy one. By the time I was born, his grandmother, mother and stepfather were all deceased. On my mother's side, her father died in 1933 several years before I was born and so, as my only living grandparent, Ann Hannah was special.

More about Ann Hannah Stickley: She was about 5ft 2in or 157cm tall, several inches shorter than any of her children or grandchildren, and was of reasonably solid build. While she could never be said to be overweight, her legs were sturdy and her feet were always firmly planted on the ground. From photos, I know that her hair was brown until she began to go grey in her late 50s. When she smiled, her face was light and somewhat mischievous, and when she was serious, her look was variously interpreted as impatient or sad or angry. In truth, I think she was probably just being serious.

She was my mother's mother. Born in central London in 1881, Ann Hannah Payne, a proud cockney, was the eighth of eleven children. In 1904, she married her first husband and became Ann Hannah White. I had never actually known the given name of her first husband, because Nana never spoke of him in my hearing, but a search of ancestry records reveals that his name was James and that his occupation was 'wine worker'. On 3 April 1904, Ann Hannah Payne and James White were married at St Marks Church, Shoreditch. They had one child, Annie May White. Sadly and tragically, James contracted consumption and died in 1907 at the age of 26, leaving Nana and her three-year-old daughter to fend for themselves in a harsh world where there was little to keep them out of the poor house. Ann Hannah worked in a laundry and continued to do that kind of work long after she married her second husband, Arthur Stickley, my grandfather, on 19 April 1908 at St Peters Church, Islington.

As self-focused as children and young adults are, it did not occur to me for many years that there was anything more to know about my grandmother than what I experienced on a day-to-day basis. Looking back on it now, it seems incredible that, after living with her for nineteen years and having a continuing relationship with her until she died when I was 45, I had never actually known her. Pondering on that fact after her death, I reminded myself that I didn't even know her first name until I was a young teenager. She was just 'Nana'. Her three daughters and sons-in-law called her 'Mum' and neighbours called her 'Mrs Stickley'. Sometimes she was referred to as 'Nana Stickley' but I never heard anyone call her Ann.

While I can say now that she was actually called Annie, I was not aware of that until a few years ago when I discovered a couple of postcards someone had written to her in London during World War I. One of them, stamped 12 February 1915, said simply:

Dear Annie,

Just a line hoping you arrived home quite safe also the children were alright. Had a letter from Arthur. Dolly managed to get work Tuesday.

From Ada & Mother.

The sad truth about names and aging is that, when a person's spouse has died and that person moves physically away from siblings and friends, there is often no one left in their circle of contacts whose place it is to address them by their first name. For the purposes of address, the person often disappears and is replaced by the role/s that they occupy in various people's lives. A poem by American woman, Donna Swanson, titled "Minnie Remembers" describes it well. Speaking of her adult children, Minnie says:

They call me "Mom" or "Mother"
or "Grandma".

Never Minnie.
My mother called me Minnie.
So did my friends.

Hank called me Minnie, too.
But they're gone.
And so is Minnie.
Only Grandma is here.
And God! She's lonely! [1]

Following my introduction to feminism in the 1970s, I often found myself thinking about the generations of women who went before me and, in particular, wondering what life had been like for my own mother and grandmother.

My mother, Lilian, was born in Holborn, London, and was nine when her family emigrated to Australia. No doubt, she would have been subjected to teasing and/or bullying by other children because of her accent and other English ways but she probably assimilated into Australian culture fairly quickly, as children do. As a teenager and young adult, I'm sure she would have been affected by the prevailing sexist attitudes toward women but, like many young women of her time, probably believed that the second-class status assigned to them could be disrupted and circumvented. Choosing the somewhat passive, unpretentious, accommodating Dave McLellan as her life's partner ensured that she would not be caught in the sexist trap, at least in her personal life. I have memories of Mum saying to us in Dad's hearing: "Girls, it's a man's world!" And Dad responding with a quick glance in my brother's direction: "But we all know who wears the pants around here, don't we?" They were both right. It was, indeed, a man's world and Mum did, indeed, "wear the pants" in our family. But it worked well for both of them and created a healthy, happy environment for us to grow up in, and for Ann Hannah to feel accepted and welcomed.

---

1   Donna Swanson (1976) 'Minnie Remembers'. In Janice Grana, (Ed). *Images: women in transition*, pp. 118–19.

Some of the circumstances of my mother's life before she married must have been painful[2] but they were things she never spoke of. After her death at age 69, I talked to her sister, Emily, about some of those issues and the picture she painted of my mother was that of 'favourite' youngest sister who enjoyed a good life as a child and teenager. Making allowances for the fact that Aunty Em's picture of Mum came through the lens of an older sister who probably felt that she did not have it quite as good as her younger sister, I nevertheless felt a degree of satisfaction at the picture she painted. My mother's experience of life, generally speaking, seems to have been positive.

Pondering on what my *grandmother's* life must have been like, however, the picture did not seem so positive. When everything is shrouded in secrecy, no doubt to protect children from having to process the painful experiences their parents and grandparents had to deal with in the past, it is nevertheless inevitable that snippets of information leak out. That's the way it was with Ann Hannah. There were indications that life had not been easy for her. So in my desire to know more about the lives of generations of women past, it was important to me to begin with a focus on the mysteries of my own grandmother's earlier life, and it is that curiosity that has resulted in the writing of this book.

I began by asking myself: What was there about my own experience of my grandmother that could assist me in my quest to get to know Ann Hannah more fully? How could I unlock the secrets, the mystery, the pain, the strengths and the victories that constituted her life? And would that even be possible almost 40 years after her death? Then I asked: What would be the best literary device to use to record her story, explore my own reactions to it and analyse it in terms of its relevance for other women?

---

2   What those circumstances were will be made clear as Ann Hannah's story unfolds in the following pages.

First, I toyed with the idea of biography. I was fairly certain that I didn't know enough about the experiences that shaped Ann Hannah's life to write a meaningful biography but, to test out that option, I set about reading, indeed, immersing myself in the biographical accounts of some of the people who interested me. More often than not, biographies are written about well-known historical figures or well-known figures in their field of influence. Some piqued my interest because there was a degree of controversy surrounding them, and others because of their focus on bringing historical figures to life.

Examples of biographies that caused controversy were those of Bob Hawke, Prime Minister of Australia from 1983–1991, written by Blanche d'Alpuget whom he later married. d'Alpuget wrote two biographies of Bob Hawke, the first *Robert J. Hawke: a Biography*,[3] and the second *Hawke, the Prime Minister*.[4] Then, following some concern about d'Alpuget's description of Bob Hawke's first wife Hazel, Sue Pieters-Hawke, daughter of Bob and Hazel, decided to write a biography of her mother in an attempt to set the record straight. *Hazel: My Mother's Story*[5] was published in the same year.

Another biography that sparked my interest, controversial because it was written against the wishes of the subject, is that by Christine Wallace who set about writing a biography of Germaine Greer. Greer made it very clear that she was not interested. She granted no interviews and, in fact, called Wallace "a dung beetle" and "flesh-eating bacterium" for persisting with the writing of her unauthorised biography, *Greer: Untamed Shrew*.[6]

3   Blanche d'Alpuget (1982) *Robert J. Hawke: a Biography*.
4   Blanche d'Alpuget (2011) *Hawke, the Prime Minister*.
5   Sue Pieters-Hawke (2011) *Hazel: My Mother's Story*.
6   Christine Wallace (1997) *Greer: Untamed Shrew*.

An excellent example of the use of biography to bring to life important historical figures is the classic feminist text by Dale Spender, *Women of Ideas (and what men have done to them): From Aphra Behn to Adrienne Rich.*[7] In the 1970s, Spender found herself wondering why history books were full of men's adventures, writing, ideas and achievements, while those of women were absent. Why had the wealth of women's common experience been submerged? "Why were women of the present cut off from women of the past and how was this achieved?"[8] The more she thought about it, the more certain she became that a great injustice had been done, that women had been deliberately ignored by historians in the interest of male dominance:

> Women's experience is non-existent, invisible, unreal from the outset, and it is my contention that if patriarchy is to be preserved, women's invisibility must remain. Obviously, this is not, for me, a state to be desired.[9]

Spender's purpose in seeking out the writings of women "from Aphra Behn to Adrienne Rich" and bringing them together in the biographical anthology, *Women of Ideas*, was to begin the process of making visible that which had been rendered invisible and to give voice to centuries of women's voices that had been silenced.

While Dale Spender's biographical accounts of women impressed and excited me, I knew that biography was not the genre with which I could do justice to my grandmother's life, so I turned my attention to the genre of psychological biography. Again, I researched this important literary technique which has proved to be invaluable in bringing a greater understanding and

---

7   Dale Spender (1982) *Women of Ideas (and what men have done to them): From Aphra Behn to Adrienne Rich.*

8   *Ibid*, p. 3.

9   *Ibid*, p. 5.

appreciation of historical figures including Louis XIII, Adolph Hitler, Bill Clinton, Elizabeth Barrett Browning, Vincent van Gogh, Mahatma Gandhi and many others. The two I chose to look at more closely were those of Bill Clinton and Vincent van Gogh.

In *In Search of Bill Clinton: A Psychological Biography*,[10] John Gartner writes about a "mildly manic character type" which he calls "Hypomanic Temperament" and, after extensive and detailed analysis of the life of United States President Bill Clinton, reaches the conclusion that ex-President Clinton is an example of Hypomanic Temperament, which Gartner defines as

> ... a mildly manic personality that imbues some people with the raw ingredients it takes to be a charismatic leader: immense energy, drive, confidence, visionary creativity, infectious enthusiasm, and a sense of personal destiny. They also have problems with impulse control, frequently in the area of sex.[11]

I cannot say that I agreed with all of Gartner's conclusions, but it was an interesting read. He states that he began his psychological study of Bill Clinton out of curiosity: "If Clinton had this mildly manic temperament, it would explain a great deal about both his strengths and weaknesses, why he is both so gifted and so flawed. This may be the first piece of the puzzle."[12] While there is neither proof nor any agreement among psychologists on the assessment of Hypomanic Temperament in relation to ex-President Clinton, it is an interesting theory resulting in a well-reasoned biography. As with all psychological biographies, however, it must be read as one among many possible explanations.

---

10 John D. Gartner (2008) *In Search of Bill Clinton: A Psychological Biography*.
11 *Ibid*, pp. 1–2.
12 *Ibid*, p. 2.

Albert J. Lubin's *Stranger on the Earth: A Psychological Biography of Vincent van Gogh*[13] is a search for the person of van Gogh through his art. Lubin, Clinical Professor of Psychiatry (Emeritus) and a practising psychoanalyst, embarked on what he called "a broad study of the relation between his [van Gogh's] psychological development and his art."[14] While Lubin focuses on van Gogh's problems and psychological conflicts, the unmistakable emphasis in his book is on the artist's ability to transform his problems into "incredible achievements."[15]

These are two examples of the ways psychological biography seeks to discover a subject through analysis of their political pronouncements, decisions, writing, behaviour or art, but I needed the focus to be more personal. Two well-known examples of psychological biography written with a view to bringing a person to life are Germaine Greer's attempt to discover her father and Drusilla Modjeska's 'search' for her mother.

Greer's book *Daddy, We Hardly Knew You*[16] has been described as a "moving, deeply personal account of Germaine Greer's impassioned search for the 'secret' truths about her father and his World War II experience." Her quest began after his death:

> Now that Daddy's need to have us not know is at an end, my need to know can be satisfied. The leads I have are few …
>
> He never referred to any kin, neither father nor mother nor sisters nor brothers nor aunts nor uncles, not even a chance anecdote. He was a man without a past.
>
> What we knew about him could be summed up in a few words.

---

13 Albert J. Lubin (1972) *Stranger on the Earth: A Psychological Biography of Vincent van Gogh*.

14 *Ibid*, p. xvii.

15 *Ibid*, p. xviii.

16 Germaine Greer (1989) *Daddy, We Hardly Knew You*.

As with Greer, Drusilla Modjeska's quest to know her mother began after her mother's death. She and her two sisters were with their mother when she died and Modjeska later wrote:

> Who was she, this woman whose death we would register in the morning? A life completed and signed for, a body handed over …
>
> My mother had died and … I did not know her, and that night, under a sky weighed down in my memory by all that had gone before, I knew that by not knowing her, I could not know myself.

Modjeska's *Poppy*[17] is referred to as a fictionalised biography: a psychological biography written in the form of fiction.

Greer's and Modjeska's works were so compelling that it confirmed for me that psychological biography was the tool that would help me in my 'search' for my grandmother. My own need to analyse and search for a greater knowledge of my grandmother does not come from a feeling that, in not knowing her, an important part of me is missing. The experience of not knowing one's grandmother is qualitatively different from that of not knowing one's mother or father. I acknowledge that knowing Nana more intimately would certainly have enriched my life, but that is not my main motivation in embarking on this search. Rather, it is to look for evidence of the personal anguish, the feelings of powerlessness, the sense of injustice that I suspect Ann Hannah experienced at certain times in her life – from the working-class struggles of her childhood, to the early death of her first husband, to the abuse perpetrated by her second husband, to life as a widow living with the family of her youngest daughter – and then to reflect on her remarkable resilience. How did she do it? How did she seemingly come out on top after all of the negatives that life had thrown at her?

---

17   Drusilla Modjeska (1990) *Poppy*.

While authors of other psychological biographies have set about to analyse their subject through their music or painting or writing or political decision-making, all I had to call on was my memory of my grandmother's words and actions. Her *actions* were very ordinary: cooking, cleaning, shopping, playing cards with her grandchildren, watching television; but some of her *sayings* struck me as being unusual. They had a quality about them that spoke to me of much deeper truths than her circumstances allowed her to reveal.

From this distance, I can say with some degree of certainty that if anyone had asked probing questions about anything she said, she would have brushed it aside as unimportant. Nevertheless, I have a suspicion that when a person does give voice to a deeply held feeling, it is often because, consciously or unconsciously, they would like to be able to tell their story. Even with careful and skilled probing, though, by a friend or therapist, some people are still not able or willing to release painful memories. The deep dark place in which their sadness and despair have been hidden for years still has a firm lock on the door. The fear of letting it out is not so much a matter of wanting to preserve their privacy as a fear for their own psychological and social stability. "What if I can't handle it? Once I start crying, I might never be able to stop." Letting go of one's deeply held emotions can be a very frightening prospect but, in many cases, when one finds the courage to do it, the relief is immeasurable.

Ann Hannah's choice not to reveal the pain of her past, however, is a perfectly legitimate one. In this age of social media where many seem to delight in sharing the intimate details of their lives online, I find myself wishing that people would hold something back for themselves. As I see it, to turn oneself inside out and lay oneself bare before whoever will listen, is to deprive oneself of an inner life, a privacy, a depth of spirit that has the capacity to bring rich meaning to one's own experience of life.

While it certainly was legitimate for Ann Hannah to choose not to reveal all of her secrets, it is also legitimate for me to want to know more in my quest to understand my relationship with my grandmother more fully.

The way I have chosen to do that here is by taking some of her sayings and analysing them with a view to uncovering the deeper meaning behind her words. Whether she uttered a particular saying several times in my hearing or only once, the emotion conveyed in some of her expressions has etched her words on my memory.

A few of the sayings I explore here have stayed with me, I'm sure, because of the cockney influence in my grandmother's expression. I begin with "'arf a cup" because this was something she said many times, and always with a mixture of seriousness and humour. Other sayings like "'e made me come (to this country)" and "'e was a wickid man" speak to me of some of the frustration and anguish she must have endured at times in her life, while "That's my Albert" allowed me to explore the depth of grief that I'm sure she experienced when her seventeen-year-old son died. "I'm a Londoner" was something I heard her say on several occasions and, while she always said it with pride, focusing on it has enabled me to enquire into what it was really like for her growing up in central London in the late nineteenth century. The final quote, "Just get on with it", points to her amazing resilience, her ability to pick herself up after any and all set-backs and get on with living a positive and fruitful life.

In addition to wanting to know my grandmother a little better, I also wanted to gain some understanding of the deep emotion that parts of her story evoked in me. Consequently, I began this project with a number of aims: to bring into view a more complete picture of Ann Hannah Stickley; to explore the depths of her private pain; to understand more fully my own emotional connection with her; to present her as representative of many women born in her time and circumstance; and to compare her many experiences with my own and those of other women today.

The exploration I embark on in this book is done respectfully and with a great amount of admiration for my grandmother's remarkable resilience.

CHAPTER ONE

"'arf a cup"

Throughout Ann Hannah's 97 years, she never lost her distinctive cockney accent. Her aitches went missing from words where they should have been and sometimes turned up where they were not meant to be. Ham and eggs, for example, would sometimes become 'am and heggs. She and my father would have fun from time to time with cockney rhyming slang: 'rubbedy dub' for pub; 'pork pies' for lies; and so on.

As a child, it never occurred to me that the way Nana spoke was different from the way the rest of us spoke. My siblings and I were used to it and so, for us, it was normal. Occasionally, I noticed that my mother would become agitated over things my grandmother said but, as a young child, I didn't understand. Once, when Mum had visitors, for example, and the adults were talking about a friend or relative, I remember Nana asking "oo?" (meaning "who"). And when she didn't get a response right away, she persisted: "oo?" Then my mother, imitating her accent, said impatiently: "Oh Mum, '*oo*'…"

As I attempt to bring Ann Hannah to life by analysing some of her sayings, I can't resist giving prominence to "'arf a cup" because it was something she often said, half seriously, half in fun.

Her love for tea was very specific. It had to be a proper cup of tea, made in a pot with a tea cosy on it. Tea bags were anathema. Before the tea leaves were placed in the pot, it had to be warmed by swirling hot water around in it and then poured out. Only then was it ready for the tea leaves and the boiling water – and the water *did* have to be boiling. She especially liked a full cup of tea, not 'arf a cup. Mostly she poured her own tea because she preferred to do it herself to ensure that the milk went in to the cup first, that she had the correct amount of milk, the exact quantity of sugar, and that the cup was full. Whenever anyone else poured her tea in line with the teachings of etiquette which say that it is bad manners to fill a tea-cup to the brim, Nana would consistently make the comment, with a kind of humorous incredulity in her voice: "'arf a cup?" This most often prompted the pourer to put etiquette aside and fill the cup to the brim.

My siblings and I still remember Nana's words and occasionally mimic her when pouring tea for each other. "'arf a cup" we say to each other, and laugh affectionately about our joint memory of her cockney accent and her insistence on a full cup of tea.

Sometimes Nana would pour her tea from the cup into her saucer and drink it from the saucer. I never understood that. If it was for the purpose of cooling it down, why didn't she simply wait for it to cool in the cup before drinking it, I wondered. It couldn't have been that she was in a hurry because she usually just sat there joining in the conversation while slowly drinking her tea from her saucer. Recently, I mentioned this to a friend who recalled that her grandparents (also from central London) used to drink from their saucers on occasions. I was so intrigued by this that I did a brief search of the history of tea-drinking in Britain and it seems that drinking tea from one's saucer was a common practice among older people in the eighteenth century. The tradition obviously continued into the nineteenth century and, for some like Ann Hannah, even into the twentieth.

From as far back as I can remember, the adults in our family practised a form of 'high tea' every afternoon, Monday to Friday. The high tea offered today in cafés and tea rooms differs markedly from the original meaning of high tea in that it usually involves delicious cakes, biscuits and/or chocolates served on two- or three-tiered plates in a leisurely atmosphere any time of the day. Originally in Britain (and in some other European countries), it was a working class tradition to serve tea in the afternoon when the working man arrived home from a hard day's work. In my family, either Mum or Nana would put the kettle on when Dad was due home from work and the three adults would sit at the kitchen table and talk about the events of the day over a cup of tea and biscuits or scones. Dinner, or 'tea' as we used to call it, came an hour or so later. Still today, I carry on my family's form of high tea in my own life (except that, I confess, I *do* use tea bags). Every day, the first thing I do when I arrive home from work is put the kettle on and relax with a cup of tea and a biscuit. The biscuit (or scone or pikelet) is not optional because, according to Ann Hannah, tea is never to be taken by itself.

A common scene when my siblings and I came home from school was Ann Hannah sitting at the kitchen table shelling peas or peeling potatoes and Mum preparing other parts of the evening meal. Mum would stop what she was doing to ensure that her children's hunger was satisfied before we went out to play, but then it was back to preparing the meal. We had our various jobs like setting the table and, afterwards, washing and drying the dishes but, mostly, we had a very easy time of it due, probably, to the fact that Mum and Nana shared the tasks between them. My mother didn't go out to work once her first child was born, so she and Ann Hannah must have had to negotiate a division of labour that satisfied them both. An easy division, once two or three of her children were on the scene, would have been that my mother had primary responsibility for everything to do with the children while my grandmother took on many of the other household chores. If that were so, that would explain why I don't have many memories of interacting on a one-to-one basis with Nana during my primary school years. I do have happy memories of sitting on the floor with her, around the radio in the days before television, listening to programs such as *Dad and Dave*. Also, she would play our favourite card games with us – grab, fish and other children's games.

As I write about "'arf a cup", I don't mean to create the impression that tea was the only beverage Ann Hannah consumed because she did enjoy soft drinks and, also, had a special use for alcohol. While I have no memory of seeing her drinking alcohol at wedding receptions or birthday celebrations when alcohol was served, I do know that she had a nip of stout from the bottle she kept in her wardrobe before going to bed every night. At some time late in her life, she changed to brandy. A bottle of stout or brandy would last her a long time and, when it was running low, she would mention it to Dad and he would buy her a bottle next time he visited the pub. Amusingly, when Nana was in her late-eighties or early-nineties and becoming more forgetful, Mum noticed that the bottle of brandy was being used up rather more quickly than previously. She also noticed that Nana sometimes appeared to be a bit tipsy! It was then that my mother hatched a plan to water down the brandy without Nana's knowledge so that the alcohol content would be diluted. One day my grandmother remarked, "I don't know what they're doing to that brandy. It's not the same as it used to be."

As a family, we always believed that it was the nip of stout or brandy that kept Nana in such good health. Only once, throughout the entire time that she lived with us, did she have an illness that necessitated medical intervention. In her mid-eighties, she reluctantly visited a doctor to have him check out her gall bladder pain. He admitted her to hospital for the purpose, I presume, of having a specialist investigate her pain with a view to surgery. According to our mother, that was the first time Nana had ever been in hospital – and she was very unhappy about it. After one or two nights in hospital, she was home again and nothing more was said about her pain, at least in the hearing of her grandchildren. She had obviously decided that surgery was not for her and she would manage on her own. In the ensuing years, I would occasionally see Nana holding her stomach and walking as if in pain, but putting up with the pain was obviously much more bearable for her than the thought of hospital and surgery.

As I thought about this particular saying in preparation for telling Ann Hannah's story, I stretched my imagination to wonder if "'arf a cup" could also symbolise something else. Could it, in fact, be a description of my grandmother's whole life? As with most people, she would have hoped for a full life but, because of some of the circumstances of her life (which will be discussed in the following pages), maybe she felt that her cup was always less than full. I am not asking was she a 'glass half full' kind of person or a 'glass half empty'? She was, without a doubt, a 'glass half full' person – always positive, always believing that things will turn out all right in the end. In fact, I don't remember Nana ever seeming depressed. She could have experienced depression from time to time, as most people do, but there was never a time when her mood created a sense of gloom in our home.

Some people do experience an overwhelming negativity at certain periods in their lives and it is often in response to situations of powerlessness or grief or a sense of meaninglessness, but I never detected that in Ann Hannah. Pondering on this, my mind went to her later years because, for some, aging with its associated physical and mental deterioration, does cause depression. I've always found the work of psychologist Erik Erikson useful. He spoke about the final stage of life in "either/or" terms and called the conflict that the healthy personality must resolve in old age, "integrity vs. despair."[18] At this final stage, he said, many people have a positive experience of integration where all the previous stages of their lives come together and they feel a sense of integrity, a sense of satisfaction with the lives they lived. They accept that aging is a natural part of life, and relax in the knowledge that they lived their lives in the best way possible. Others have a negative experience akin to despair. Such people look back over their lives and wish things could have been different but realise that it is too late to make changes. Sadly, the regret and self-blame that they feel are often expressed in a need to blame others.

As I saw it, Ann Hannah displayed no signs of experiencing despair in her old age. On the contrary, it was as if she had consciously looked back over her long and eventful life and said, "I've had some rough patches but, overall, I've done well." While I have no way of knowing if she *did* consciously look back and evaluate her life, such a response would have been in tune with her positive attitude to life. She certainly did have some rough patches, not the least of which would have been the death of her first husband three years into their marriage. In fact, in a rare moment of reminiscence with my sister, Bev, she declared that her first husband was the only man she ever loved. While life was difficult at times, she made the best of the situation life handed her and went on to live a happy and productive life.

In many ways, Ann Hannah was dealt "'arf a cup" but, through courage and determination, she made sure that her cup was as full as it could be.

---

18   Erik H. Erikson (1980) *Identity and the Life Cycle*, pp. 104–5.

CHAPTER TWO

"I'm a Londoner"

Ann Hannah was proud of her cockney roots. I remember a conversation in my early teenage years when I asked her what 'cockney' actually meant and she began by saying that Londoners who were born and lived within the sound of the Bow Bells were called cockney. She went on to explain that there was a church in the centre of London (which I later discovered was the Church of St Mary-le-Bow), and anyone who lived within about a mile of the church, she said, could hear the church bells whenever they rang. Those people were seen to be the 'real' Londoners, the cockneys, and they were mostly working-class and lower-income families. I later learned that 'cockney' began as a term of derision. As long ago as the sixteenth century, travel writer Fynes Moryson (1566–1630) wrote: "Londoners, and all within the sound of the Bow Bells, are in reproach called Cockneys."[19]

The cockney accent was, for a long time, judged to be inferior to other modes of speech in the English language. Indeed, a report written by The Conference on the Teaching of English in London Elementary Schools and issued by the London County Council in 1909, declared that

---

19 <www.dailymail.co.uk/.../Bow-Bells-mark-area-true-Londoners-drowned-capitals-noise>

> ... the Cockney mode of speech, with its unpleasant twang, is a
> modern corruption without legitimate credentials, and is unworthy
> of being the speech of any person in the capital city of the Empire.[20]

While there were, at the same time, comments in defence of cockney, the fact that the only accent to be heard on the British Broadcasting Corporation (BBC) for many decades was "Received Pronunciation" (RP, also called the Queen's English, Oxford English or BBC English) shows that the rejection of cockney English by mainstream Britain continued right up until recent times. Toward the end of the twentieth century, there was a noticeable change in BBC programming and, while surveys revealed that most people still preferred RP, the cockney accent was increasing in popularity. While it cannot be said, even today, that the cockney mode of speech is welcomed by a majority in Britain, it is at least tolerated in a way that was not evident when Ann Hannah lived there. A recent documentary on ABC television's *Foreign Correspondent* highlighted the fact that, due to the massive numbers of immigrants settling in London's East End, the traditional Anglo-cockney population is now in the minority.[21] It is my hope that cockney culture will not disappear altogether but, rather, that the blend of traditional Anglo-cockneys and new immigrants will work in a positive way to produce a new and vibrant culture.

During an overseas trip in the 1970s, I purposely included London in my travel plans because I wanted to search for the area where my grandmother grew up. While I didn't manage to get there on that trip, I did take home some postcards of the

---

20   London County Council (1909), <https://ifind.swan.ac.uk/discover/
     Record/579503>
21   'Foreign Correspondent'. 26 August 2016, <www.abc.net.au/foreign/
     content>

Church of St Mary-le-Bow. When I showed Nana the postcards and talked to her about the bells that I believed had been really significant in her early life in London, she seemed not to recognise the old church, nor to understand what I was talking about. Was it because she was 93 years of age and her memory was failing? Was it because the church was so different after its reconstruction following the bombing that partially destroyed it in May 1941? Or was it that she had never, in fact, seen the church? It is possible, even probable, that she had grown up within the sound of the Bow Bells but had never actually been there.

In 1996, long after Ann Hannah's death, when I was in Brighton attending a conference, I decided to try once again to visit London and look for the Church of St Mary-le-Bow. The image I have always had in my mind of central London when my grandmother was a girl, is that portrayed at the beginning of the movie *My Fair Lady*, when Audrey Hepburn as the cockney flower girl Eliza Doolittle was selling flowers in a market place in the centre of London: an image of poverty, hunger and hopelessness. I knew everything would be very different in London after so many years but, still, that image and my belief that my own grandmother had probably lived in those circumstances had stayed with me.

As it turns out, a search of several decades of the UK Census has led me to the conclusion that, while her family was probably poor, it was not the kind of abject poverty portrayed in the movie. Rather, her family would probably more correctly be classified as 'the working poor'. It seems that her father, my great-grandfather William Payne, worked as a carpenter and, with the help of other members of the family, was probably able to support my great-grandmother Emma Payne, and their eleven children, but it was most likely a frugal existence. In addition to having primary responsibility for the children, Emma Payne is listed as being self-employed as a pipe-cover liner.[22]

William Payne died in 1896 leaving his wife, Emma, to support the children who were still living at home. Each of the eleven children seems to have had employment of one kind or another after they reached a certain age. According to the 1891 Census, the six older children were in employment, the next three (including Ann Hannah) were listed as "scholars" and the two youngest aged four and two, were not yet in school.

The 1901 Census shows that, by then, there were only five children remaining at home and their mother, Emma Payne, is listed as "head". All but the youngest had employment, and Ann Hannah's employment is listed as "laundry worker."

My memory of our childhood in Brisbane is that our grandmother was always careful to avoid waste due, in all probability, to the fact that she grew up in difficult financial circumstances and/or was conscious of all the poverty around her. However, my siblings and I could never bring ourselves to empathise with "the starving children of England" every time she tried to shame us into eating all of the food on our plates at mealtimes. It was then the 1940s and 1950s when, regardless of the expense of fighting and then recovering from two world wars, England's economy had surely begun to improve. While there certainly would still have been many families living in poverty, the welfare system would have ensured that there were far fewer "poor starving children" than when Nana lived there in the late nineteenth and early twentieth centuries.

---

22 My research has not enlightened me as to what a pipe-cover liner actually did, but it was likely to be something Ann Hannah's mother could do at home while also tending to the needs of her large family.

Other examples of Ann Hannah's careful attitude toward money come to mind. One day, when my grandmother and I were the only ones at home, the Salvation Army came knocking on the door seeking a donation to support their work. Nana was downstairs in the laundry and I was upstairs in the house. As the Salvation Army worker walked up the front stairs, Nana called out to me in a loud voice, "Betty, give the Salvation Army sixpence." I can still feel my embarrassment at the fact that, even back then, sixpence seemed such a paltry amount. But I duly went to the drawer where Mum kept some coins and took out sixpence. I wonder if the worker, who graciously thanked me for my generosity, noticed the embarrassment on my face.

Then there was something Ann Hannah used to do every year when we arrived at our usual camping area at Currumbin Beach on the Gold Coast for our annual holiday. The area was full of families in tents or caravans and only one toilet/shower block to service us all. Every year, after Nana's first visit to the toilet, she would come back with a roll of toilet paper that she had stolen from the public toilets. On arrival back at our tent, she would produce it from the place where she had carried it surreptitiously and then put it in a safe place in her corner of the tent. On every visit to the toilet thereafter, she would tear some off and take it in her pocket. There was no doubt that she did this out of fear of ever going to the toilet block and finding that there was no paper, but it was something that always riled my mother: "Mum, we can afford to buy a roll of toilet paper to keep in the tent. You don't have to steal it." But, every year, the ritual was repeated.

Continuing the story of my quest to find the church of St Mary-le-Bow, when I set out again during my 1996 visit to London, I had no idea what the area would be called 80 years on, but my determination gave me confidence that I would be successful provided the church was still standing after two world wars.

I realised, too, that there was a strong possibility that this incredibly significant historic site could already have been destroyed to make way for commercial enterprises, but I pressed on. In my search, I asked several people where I might find the Church of St Mary-le-Bow – taxi drivers, bus drivers, police – but they were not able to help. Eventually, I found my way to the district of Cheapside where, after more enquiries, I was directed to an old church dwarfed by commercial buildings all around. Why was I so surprised? I guess I still had a picture planted firmly in my mind of a huge Church complete with steeple, with bells that rang out across the countryside: a central feature of the landscape. It was not so.

I felt cheated and somewhat sad but, when I stepped inside and walked slowly through the old church, it was impossible to avoid feeling the history of the place and, as strange as it may seem, I felt particularly close to my grandmother. I did not imagine for one moment that she had attended services there because she never did show any interest in, or inclination toward, religious or spiritual matters. But I was strangely aware that I was in a place that had real significance in my family's history. While I was there, the bells rang out and, at that moment, I found myself choked up with emotion. The feeling of closeness I was experiencing was one of the few emotional connections I ever had with my grandmother because of the overwhelmingly practical focus of our relationship. This, therefore, was a precious moment.

Looking back on it, I wonder what my emotional response would have been if I had known at the time that these were not the actual bells my grandmother used to hear. Much of the church, I learned later, was destroyed during the Blitz of London in 1941 and the bells Nana used to hear crashed to the ground and were totally destroyed. Restoration of the church was delayed until 1956 and the bells were not heard again until 1961. Even if

I had known all of that, I think I would still have been moved by the significance of the moment.

Ann Hannah in Her Social Context

Thinking of Ann Hannah as a Londoner living within the sound of the Bow Bells, and reminding myself of her concern for the 'starving children of England', prompted me to look into the social and political context in which my grandmother lived in her early years.

According to UK Census records, William J. Payne was born in Westminster around 1843 and Emma A. Payne (nee Smith) in Clerkenwell around 1849. Several of the children, including Ann Hannah, were also born in Clerkenwell. It seems that the family moved, at some stage, to Shoreditch, though when that occurred is not clear. What is clear is that Ann Hannah was married to James White (her first husband) on 3 April 1904 in the parish of Shoreditch St Mark.

Clerkenwell

Clerkenwell was an area of Central London in the Borough of Islington. In 1900, it became part of the Metropolitan Borough of Finsbury. *Clerken* is the plural of *clerk* which is a variant of *clerc*, meaning literate person or cleric or clergyman. Clerkenwell was named for Clerks' Well and, apparently, part of it is still visible today through a window of a building called Wells Court on Farringdon Lane.

In the seventeenth and eighteenth centuries, Clerkenwell was a thriving commercial and industrial centre. The Industrial Revolution (eighteenth and nineteenth centuries) saw the establishment of breweries, distilleries and the printing industry. Witherbys, Europe's oldest printing company, was established in Clerkenwell in 1740. Many people in the region were employed in Clerkenwell's clock-and watch-making industries, including Ann Hannah's oldest brother, William. Jewellery-making, too, was a flourishing industry.

Clerkenwell was home to the wealthy and, also, to the very poor. Oliver Cromwell once owned a house on Clerkenwell Close, as did several aristocrats. In contrast, Clerkenwell Green was the setting for Charles Dickens's *Oliver Twist*, where the Artful Dodger taught Oliver his pickpocketing skills among the wealthy shoppers attending the busy markets.

Shoreditch

About one mile from Clerkenwell was the parish of Shoreditch. In 1899, it became the Metropolitan Borough of Shoreditch and then much later, in1965, it was incorporated into the London Borough of Hackney.

Shoreditch has a rich history as a centre of entertainment. In the sixteenth century, England's first playhouse known as 'The Theatre' was built in Shoreditch. Some of Shakespeare's plays were performed at The Theatre and, also, at nearby Curtain Theatre. In the late nineteenth century, the National Standard Theatre on Shoreditch High Street was one of the largest theatres in London. The London Music Hall was built at 95–99 Shoreditch High Street in 1856, was rebuilt in 1894 and remained until 1935. The Music Hall's records show that Charlie Chaplin performed there in the days before he achieved fame in America.[23] I don't know if Ann Hannah ever actually saw him perform or if it was through his movies that she was familiar with him, but Charlie Chaplin was always one of her favourites.

Shoreditch had become a centre for the textile and furniture industries during the eighteenth and nineteenth centuries but,

---

23 Walter Thornbury (1873) 'Shoreditch', *Old and New London: Volume 2*, pp. 194–195.

by the end of the nineteenth century, that is, by the time Ann Hannah lived there, both industries were in serious decline and Shoreditch had developed a reputation for crime, prostitution and poverty.

In my attempts to uncover the social conditions that existed during my grandmother's early life, I have focused my attention on two issues: the economic situation of her family and general attitudes toward women.

Economic Situation

The most helpful description of the economic diversity found in London at the end of the nineteenth century is that by Charles Booth in his *Life and Labour of the People in London*.[24] In this work, Booth sets out a list of class descriptions that has helped me develop a better understanding of the economic circumstances of Ann Hannah's family of origin. If her father, William Payne, had regular work as a carpenter, then the family would qualify for Booth's classification: "Regular standard earnings ... fairly comfortable". If, however, he did not have regular work but, rather, was a labourer in the building trade (rather than a carpenter), he may have worked, as Booth states, "only eight or nine months in a year", in which case the family's economic situation would have been dire at times.

Given that William Payne's occupation is listed as 'carpenter' in the 1891 UK Census, it is probably safe to assume that he had "regular standard earnings" and that the family lived relatively comfortably. In discussing this particular class category, Booth adds – "As a rule the wives do not work, but the children do: the boys commonly following the father, the girls taking local trades

24   Charles Booth (1902) *Life and Labour of the People in London*, pp. 33–62.

or going out to service."[25] It seems, then, that Ann Hannah's focus on the "poor starving children of England" did not come as a result of her own experience but, rather, of her knowledge of the situation of other children she had known or known about. While it does appear that her experience was nothing like that of an extreme Eliza Doolittle kind of poverty, she nevertheless grew up with the imperative common to working-class families – that waste must be avoided at all times.

Attitudes toward Women

Writing in 1869, approximately twelve years before Ann Hannah was born, philosopher and economist John Stuart Mill argued that

> … the principle which regulates the existing social relations between the two sexes – the legal subordination of one sex to the other – is wrong in itself, and now one of the chief hindrances to human improvement.[26]

When Mill wrote in *The Subjection of Women* that "the law should be no respecter of persons, but should treat all alike,"[27] he painted a picture of what it must have been like for women living in a situation of legal inferiority to men. He railed against the doctrine which held that "men have a right to command and women are under an obligation to obey, … that men are fit for government and women unfit …"[28] He likened women's situation to that of slavery and spoke of a "system of privilege and enforced subjection [which has] its yoke tightly riveted on the necks of those who are kept down by it …" [29]

---

25 *Ibid*, pp. 33–62.
26 John Stuart Mill (1970) *The Subjection of Women*, p.3.
27 *Ibid*, p. 4.
28 *Ibid*, p. 4.
29 *Ibid*. p. 13.

More than a century later, feminist and socialist Elizabeth Wilson revealed that, while the situation had changed somewhat, women in the 1970s were still socialised to accept a position of inferiority and to be 'happy' serving their husbands and children.

> Women ... are reared almost from birth, certainly from early childhood, to conceive of happiness and emotional fulfillment in terms of their future relationship with husband and children.[30]

She wrote that "social policies discriminate against ... women", that pay structures and the law "deny women a place in society equal to that of men", and that "the legal system continues to define women as the dependents of men in many areas of life".[31]

Articles from the middle of the nineteenth century, quoted by Wilson, discuss the fact that, while the Industrial Revolution brought with it advantages for single women and widows, it created a double workload for married women. Since there was an abundance of profitable employment, young women were no longer "driven into an early marriage by the necessity of seeking a home."[32] Similarly, widows were not driven into early re-marriage. Writing in 1863 about the situation in Lancashire, Ellen Barlee observed that when the mills closed at midday on Saturday, the men and the single women came out on the town, making it "a gala day." But for married women, the abundance of work meant that they were forced to fill two roles. When their work at the mills ceased each Saturday, their huge workload as wife and mother began.

> The married women, who seem the slaves of Lancashire society, are obliged then ... to set to work harder than ever. They have only this day to clean their house, provide for the week, bake for the family, mend clothes, besides doing any washing that is not put out and

---

30   Elizabeth Wilson (1977) *Women and the Welfare State*, p. 9.

31   *Ibid.* p. 8.

32   W. Hickson (1840) *Handloom Weavers Report*, p. 44.

attend the market to purchase the Sunday's dinner … Then there is also washing the children and setting them to rights, always the Saturday night's business in every cottage – so that the poor mother seldom gets a rest ere the Sabbath dawns if indeed she is not up all night.[33]

For many, the stress of the constant requirement to fill two roles was exacerbated by the situation of legal subordination of women to men described by John Stuart Mill which meant that women were subject to the whims and moods of their husbands at all times. If a man was violent toward his wife and/or children, for example, a woman had no legal recourse. Most simply put up with the violence because, as Mill pointed out, to complain would often provoke more violence:

There is never any want of women who complain of ill-usage by their husbands. There would be infinitely more, if complaint were not the greatest of all provocatives to a repetition and increase of the ill-usage.[34]

If a woman did find the courage to take her case to court, she would inevitably be placed back under the domination of her husband. This, in Mill's view, was a situation of extreme injustice:

In no other case (except that of a child) is the person who has been proved judicially to have suffered an injury, replaced under the physical power of the culprit who inflicted it.[35]

Concern about the subordinate status of women and the total powerlessness some women experienced in their marriages caused some researchers and writers to delve into history for answers to their questions about how and when the situation of male superiority began. To their surprise, they discovered that it had

---

33   Ellen Barlee. *A Visit to Lancashire in December 1862*. Quoted in Wilson (1977), p. 21.
34   Mill (1970), pp. 15–16.
35   *Ibid.* p. 16.

not always been thus. Charlotte Stopes, writing in 1894, spoke of the ancient rights in which women had enjoyed much more power and freedom. Such rights, she said, were evident as recently as the seventeenth and eighteenth centuries but, by the nineteenth century, women had been systematically reduced to a position subordinate to men in every way.[36]

Women in the more privileged classes were expected to focus first on snaring a husband and, then, to finding fulfilment through the lives of their husbands and children. They were to have no ambition for themselves but to be totally happy with lives of idleness. Florence Nightingale, who resisted all attempts by her parents to push her into marriage, wrote at length about the 'woman question'.[37] From her own experience of forced 'leisure', she described the experience of being "shut up tight within the conventions which forbade independent action to a woman."[38]

Cicely Hamilton writing in 1909, described marriage as a 'trade'. Introducing the 1981 edition of Hamilton's book, Jane Lewis outlines Hamilton's view that "girls are trained to make themselves pleasing to men because marriage is the primary way for women to earn their living."[39] While men have a degree of choice in selecting the trade by which they earn their living, Hamilton wrote, women have no such choice. A man is encouraged to work and increase his ability to purchase property and goods, but the only thing a woman is required to do is

> ... enkindle and satisfy the desire of the male, who would thereupon admit her to such share of the property he possessed or earned as

---

36 Charlotte Carmichael Stopes (1894) *British Freewomen: Their Historic Privilege*. Discussed in Spender (1982), p. 386.

37 Florence Nightingale (1979) 'Cassandra'. In Ray Strachey. *The Cause*. First published in 1928, pp. 395-418.

38 Nightingale, quoted in Spender (1982), p. 400.

39 Cicely Hamilton (1981) *Marriage as a Trade*. First published in 1909, p. 1.

should seem good to him. In other words, she exchanged, by the ordinary process of barter, possession of her person for the means of existence.[40]

In addition to the expectation on women in the more privileged classes that they trade their bodies and reproductive capacities for the practical means of existence bestowed on them by their husbands, they were also required to assert that they were happy:

> That it is obligatory for a woman to be happy, to present a contented and cheerful disposition to her master in order that he can feel satisfied with the arrangement and secure in the knowledge of his own psychological (as well as financial) indispensability, is a lesson that mothers unwaveringly teach their daughters...[41]

In the lower classes, the requirement for women to be 'happy' (or, at least, to refrain from complaining about their lot in life) was similar. From snippets my sisters and I had been able to glean over the years, it became clear that our grandmother was not happy in her marriage, but that no avenue of official complaint was available to her even though her second husband Arthur Stickley, our grandfather, was physically and sexually violent in the home. The fact that women were still legally subordinate to men in those early years of the twentieth century meant that Nana had no recourse. There was nothing she could do but put up with the situation and do all within her power to protect her children.[42]

Closely related to social context is the political context in which my grandmother lived. While I believe she would have been largely oblivious to the political machinations going on around

---

40 *Ibid.* pp. 26–27.
41 Spender (1982), pp. 400–01.
42 Ann Hannah's 'nightmare' of a relationship is pursued more fully in
    Chapters Three and Four.

her, the late nineteenth and early twentieth centuries were very interesting political times in the United Kingdom, especially for women.

Women's Suffrage

A concerted effort to gain better working conditions for women was underway during Ann Hannah's early years. The fight for women's suffrage increased in intensity from her childhood years until, at least, the beginning of the First World War, but she never spoke of these things to her grandchildren. Historically, politics had always been the domain of rich and powerful men and, while Liberal governments were intent on extending suffrage to more and more men, but not to women, an increasing number of women were determined to change the status quo. The general view in political parties and in the community was that women did not belong in politics and that decisions of national and international importance were best left to men. It occurred to me to wonder how Ann Hannah and her parents and siblings would have felt about that situation but, in all probability, the majority of working-class men and women would have accepted the status quo without question. In every generation, the need to focus on earning enough money to keep one's family fed and clothed day after day usually precludes the luxury of philosophical and political analysis.

This is not to say that there were no demands for justice by the workers of Britain. By the late 1880s, unskilled and semi-skilled workers were becoming organised. They fought for better working conditions, higher wages and the right to organise. In 1888, for example, there were 1,400 women out on strike at the Bryant and May matchstick factory in protest against poor wages and dangerous conditions.[43]

---

43   <http://www.spartacus.schoolnet.co.uk/TUmatchgirls.htm>

While the campaign for women's suffrage in the latter part of the nineteenth century was waged mainly by middle- and upper-class women, a growing number of working-class women, politicised by the fight for better working conditions, were also calling for the right to vote. Selina Cooper, a working-class woman and activist in Lancashire, explained why it was important to her that working women be granted the right to vote. Women, she said,

> ... do not want their political power to enable them to boast that they are on equal terms with the men. They want to use it for the same purpose as men, to get better conditions ... Every woman in England is longing for her political freedom in order to make the lot of the worker pleasanter and to bring about reforms which are wanted.[44]

Suffragists in the north of England launched a petition on May Day 1900 aimed directly at women cotton workers in Lancashire. After one year, they had obtained 29,359 signatures and, in 1902, a delegation of women textile workers was able to present a petition of 37,000 signatures to Parliament, demanding votes for women.[45]

While more and more women were being mobilised, it was clear to them that the issue of votes for women held little interest for their male counterparts. Hannah Mitchell, a working-class suffragist, lamented the fact that there was very little support for women's issues among the male members of the Independent Labour Party. Of the socialist men, she said:

> Even as socialists they seldom translate their faith into words, being still conservatives at heart, especially where women are concerned.

---

44   <http://www.socialistparty.org.uk/socialistwomen/sw9.htm>
45   <http://www.bbc.co.uk/radio4/womanshour/timeline/1900.shtml>

> Most of us who married found that 'votes for women' were of less interest to our husbands than their own dinners.[46]

The movement for women's suffrage did have a degree of support among male politicians. In fact, Bills calling for voting rights to be extended to women were presented in Parliament but, each time (1870, 1886 and 1897), the Bill was defeated.

After years of campaigning, women were becoming impatient. The London Society for Women's Suffrage, formed in 1867, campaigned vigorously for the right to vote.[47] Women in Lancashire and many other places had organised around the issue of women's suffrage. Lydia Becker founded the Manchester Women's Suffrage Committee followed, in October 1903, by the establishment of the Women's Social and Political Union (WSPU) by Emmeline Pankhurst. Mrs Pankhurst, her daughter Christabel and many other women had, until then, put their faith in the Independent Labour Party (ILP) and the trade unions but, when it became clear that the majority of men in the ILP and trade unions were lukewarm on the issue of women's suffrage, they broke away and formed their own Union, the WSPU.

Hopes were raised momentarily when the Liberal Party of Herbert Henry Asquith came to power in Britain in 1906 because members of the WSPU believed that liberalism, by its very nature, would support women's political rights. When this proved not to be the case, the actions of the WSPU became more militant.

One of their tactics was to disrupt public addresses by politicians. For example, Christabel Pankhurst and Annie Kenney deliberately flouted social convention by attending a gathering in Manchester that was addressed by Winston Churchill and Sir Edward Grey.[48] Contrary to conventional courtesies, Pankhurst

---

46   <http://www.socialistparty.org.uk/socialistwomen/sw9.htm>
47   <www.learningcurve.gov.uk>
48   Such political events were usually 'men-only' affairs so it was unusual and,

and Kenney began heckling the speakers, interrupting and calling on the speakers to state their position on the issue of women's political rights. Toward the end of the meeting, they stood and held up a banner calling for "Votes for Women". In an effort to silence them, the police arrested them on a trumped-up charge of 'technical assault on a policeman', and both were fined. Rather than pay the fine, however, they chose to go to prison hoping that such a tactic would bring more widespread attention to their cause.

Frustrated by the lack of success such tactics brought, the WSPU became even more militant: marching in the street, chaining themselves to railings, breaking windows, physically attacking politicians and damaging property owned by the church and other institutions judged by them to be supporting the continued dominance of men over women. Many women suffered physical and sexual abuse by police as they were arrested and thrown into prison. In prison, they engaged in hunger strikes with the aim of causing maximum embarrassment to the government.

Emmeline Pankhurst herself was arrested seven times before the vote was won. Her three daughters, Christabel, Adela and Sylvia, also spent time in prison for their activism. Following one period of six weeks in prison, Emmeline Pankhurst spoke out about the conditions she and others had to endure: solitary confinement, vermin, lack of food, all of which she called "civilised torture."[49] Nevertheless, she remained undaunted. In one of her court appearances, Mrs Pankhurst declared: "We are here not because we are law-breakers; we are here in our effort to become law-makers."[50]

---

no doubt, uncomfortable for the men to see women in the audience.
49   Paula Bartley (2002) *Emmeline Pankhurst*, p. 103.
50   *Ibid,* p. 100.

In 1911, British writer and feminist Ethel Smyth composed the stirring feminist anthem 'The March of the Women' and dedicated it to Emmeline Pankhurst and the WSPU. The anthem is still available today, more than 100 years later:

Shout, shout, up with your song!
Cry with the wind, for the dawn is break-ing;
March, march, swing you a-long,
Wide blows our ban-ner, and hope is wa-king.
Song with its sto-ry, dreams with their glo-ry
Lo! they call, and glad is their word!
Loud and lou-der it swells,
Thun-der of free-dom, the voice of the Lord!

Long, long – we in the past
Cowered in dread from the light of heaven,
Strong, strong – stand we at last,
Fearless in faith and with sight new given.
Strength with its beauty, Life with its duty,
(Hear the voice, oh hear and obey!)
These, these – beckon us on!
Open your eyes to the blaze of day.

Comrades – ye who have dared
First in the battle to strive and sorrow!
Scorned, spurned – nought have ye cared,
Raising your eyes to a wider morrow,
Ways that are weary, days that are dreary,
Toil and pain by faith ye have borne;
Hail, hail – victors ye stand,
Wearing the wreath that the brave have worn!

Life, strife – those two are one,
Naught can ye win but by faith and daring.
On, on – that ye have done
But for the work of to-day preparing.
Firm in reliance, laugh a defiance,
(Laugh in hope, for sure is the end)

March, march – many as one,
Shoulder to shoulder and friend to friend.[51]

As determined as the women were to gain the vote at the beginning of the twentieth century, the Asquith Liberal government was just as determined to refuse their demands. Consequently, their demonstrations were met with brutal repression. The government's response to the hunger strikes was to order the horrendous torture of force-feeding. Then, in 1913, the Asquith government passed the Prisoners (Temporary Discharge for Ill Health) Act, better known by its nickname: The Cat and Mouse Act. This Act allowed the women in prison to go on hunger strikes and, as their health deteriorated, they could be released on the grounds of ill health, only to be re-arrested a short time later. In prison once again, they would continue their hunger strike, their health would deteriorate further, they would be released again, then re-arrested. And so it went on. While the government hoped these stringent measures would be an effective weapon against women's civil disobedience and determination to gain the power of the vote, such tactics inflicted untold damage on the health of the women involved.

As a feminist committed to the militancy and outspokenness of Second Wave feminism,[52] I am full of admiration for those

---

51   These words have been copied exactly as they appeared on the original sheet of music with the same capitals, hyphens, and other punctuation, <http://www.sandscapepublications.com/intouch/marchwords.html> Also available on YouTube, <http://www.youtube.com/watch?v=LCtGkCg7trY>

52   Second Wave is the name given to the Women's Liberation Movement that began in the West in the 1960s. First Wave feminism is identified as that which started in the United States with the Seneca Falls women's rights convention in 1848, energised by the activism of women like Elizabeth Cady Stanton and Susan B. Anthony. In the late 1980s, when the strong and determined activism of Second Wave feminism had subsided, there was an attempt to identify a Third Wave but, since the

women who fought without thought for their own wellbeing so that I and all women in many parts of the world today are in a position to take the vote for granted. We accept without question that it is our right as adults to have equal say with men in the government of our country. If the fight for the right to vote were happening today, I know I would be at the forefront of the battle. But I cannot help wondering where Ann Hannah was when all of those demonstrations were actually happening during her years as a teenager and young adult in London.

When we were growing up, our grandmother had no stories to tell us about the situation of women during her early years in London, nor about women marching in the streets, nor the civil disobedience of women demanding the right to vote, nor their being arrested and imprisoned. One would think that she would have read about it in the newspapers or heard her parents and older siblings discussing it from time to time. I wonder if it was because none of us ever gave her the chance to talk about herself and her own experiences. After all, she was an 'add-on' in our home and, therefore, obviously did not warrant much

---

Third Wave (influenced by postmodernism) was presented as a more conciliatory and less angry brand of feminism, women committed to Second Wave feminist values of social justice and human rights for all, continue that fight today. It should be noted that identifying 'waves' of the feminist movement was an invention of feminists in Western countries, but that does not mean that feminism was confined to the West. Ranjana Kumari, in her brief history of feminism in India, for example, refers to 'phases' of the women's movement from 1850 to the present. Ranjana Kumari. (2016) 'A Brief History of Indian Feminism (1850–1995),' <https://www.globalcitizen.in/en/content/ranjana-kumari-a-brief-history-of-indian-feminism/>

Begum Rokeya Hossain of Bangladesh was writing about women's issues as early as 1905 and, in 1916, founded the Muslim Women's Association. The push for women's liberation is a global movement with a long and proud history, <http://nationalwomansparty.org/womenwecelebrate/begum-rokeya-sakhawat-hossain/>

attention from self-focused children and teenagers. Or maybe it was because the demands of the suffragists, their activism and treatment by police and politicians did not register in her mind at the time as having any relevance to her immediate life.

This was certainly the case for the majority of women when Second Wave feminism was at its most active in the 1970s and 1980s. Gisela Kaplan, in *The Meagre Harvest: The Australian Women's Movement 1950s–1990s* says that, even at the height of Second Wave feminism in western Europe, only "about one per cent of adult women were said to be core participants, with an additional five to twenty per cent joining in on single issues …"[53] With reference to the Australian situation, she said: "It is hard to judge how many women actually joined the movement because of its informal and spontaneous nature,"[54] but suggested that the numbers were relatively small. Even with the small numbers, however, she goes on to say that the Australian women's movement was characterised by "an indomitable spirit and an unparalleled tenacity,"[55] For those of us who were involved, our activism was central to our lives but, for the vast majority of women, if they noticed at all, it was certainly largely peripheral to their everyday living.

It is possible that the media in Britain in the late nineteenth and early twentieth centuries only focused on the actions and subsequent arrests of high profile, middle-and upper-class women, adding to working-class women's perception that the campaign for votes for women had no relevance to them. If that were true, it would have been in spite of Sylvia Pankhurst having devoted many years to helping motivate working-class women to

---

53 Gisela Kaplan (1996) *The Meagre Harvest: The Australian Women's Movement 1950s–1990s*, p. 61. See also Gisela Kaplan (1992) *Contemporary Western European Feminism*.

54 *Ibid*, p. 61.

55 *Ibid*, p. 62.

become involved. Even as she demonstrated alongside her mother Emmeline and sister Christabel as a member of the WSPU, demanding that the right to vote be extended to women, Sylvia's focus as a socialist was on the rights of working women:

> I wanted to rouse these women of the submerged masses to be, not merely the argument for more fortunate people, but to be fighters on their own account despising mere platitudes and catch cries, revolting against the hideous conditions about them, and demanding for themselves and their families a full share in the benefits of civilisation and progress.[56]

In 1904, Sylvia Pankhurst helped organise a march for jobs that saw 1000 people march from London's East End to Westminster. Questioning the growing militancy of the WSPU, Sylvia believed that what was needed was "not more serious militancy of the few but a stronger appeal to the great masses to join in the struggle." Her appeal was to the people, particularly the women, from London's East End. In January 1914, the East London Federation of the WSPU pulled away from the WSPU and formed its own independent organisation, the East London Federation of Suffragettes (ELFS). When war broke out later that year, Emmeline and Christabel Pankhurst put their energies into supporting the British war effort while Sylvia Pankhurst, a pacifist, continued her fight for women's suffrage and for better wages and working conditions for the women brought into factories to replace the men who had gone off to war.

If it is true, as I suspect, that Ann Hannah had little or no knowledge of the political dramas going on around her, the commitment of the suffragists and especially of Sylvia Pankhurst and others who chose to focus on the plight of working-class women, would surely have had a positive effect on her life as a worker and as a woman. Regarding the vote, however, my grand-

---

56   <http://www.marxist.com/sylvia-pankhurst.htm>

mother never had the opportunity to vote in her home country of Britain. She and her family emigrated to Australia in 1921 and it was "not until 1928 that all women over twenty-one were finally enfranchised" in Britain.[57]

I have often wished I had been able to have conversations with Ann Hannah to ascertain what she *did* know about the courageous activism of the suffragists in her home country in her early years, but that had not been possible. My own introduction to feminist history and activism came during my time of study in the United States in the 1970s and, by the time I returned home at the end of 1977, Nana was already 96 years old and died the following year. What I do know is that, while she gave no indication of feminist knowledge or involvement, she did live her life in both London and Australia as a strong, determined woman.

---

57   <http://www.socialistparty.org.uk/socialistwomen/sw9.htm>

CHAPTER THREE

"I never wanted to come (to this country) 'e made me come"

Ann Hannah arrived in Australia in 1921 with husband, Arthur Stickley, and her four children: Annie May White (daughter of her first marriage) age seventeen, Emily, eleven, Lilian, my mother, nine and Albert, six. They came as "assisted immigrants".

It is difficult to imagine what it must have been like to pull up roots in one's home country and travel by ship to the other side of the world, knowing that there would never be an opportunity to return. Arthur would probably have seen it as a chance to escape the memories of war-torn England and look for opportunities in a new country; the children would have approached it with mixed emotions – sadness at having to leave their friends behind but excitement about a new adventure. Ann Hannah, it seems, resented the fact that she had been forced to leave family and friends and travel by ship with four children to a foreign land. It was not her decision. In fact, her opinion had not been sought and her wishes not considered. As is so often the case when a person is confronted with the inevitable, however, she resigned herself to coping with whatever came her way. She would have endured the loneliness and the sadness at having been cut adrift from her mother, siblings, extended family, and the many things that had, until then, given her life meaning.

The evidence supporting the conclusion I have drawn so confidently comes from my memory of something I heard Ann Hannah say: "I never wanted to come. 'e made me come." Sometimes my father and grandmother would exchange banter about all kinds of topics and, in the style adopted by many Australian working-class men, Dad would stretch the humour a bit too far and say things like: "Why did you come here then, if you don't like our country?" Or, "Why don't you go back to where you came from then?" His mother-in-law would usually respond with something equally risky like: "I wish I could. At least, I wouldn't 'ave to put up with the likes of you." Then, they would laugh and get on with what they were each doing.

One day, however, when Dad said something like: "Why did you come here then?" Nana's mood changed and she responded thoughtfully and sadly: "I never wanted to come. 'e made me come." I remember it very clearly. I was in the room, not involved in the exchanges between the adults but enjoying the light-hearted atmosphere as I went about whatever I was doing. I was a child, not yet a teenager, but I remember well when the atmosphere changed. It was as if my father's remark that day had triggered something in my grandmother that was deep and painful. I was too young to understand or even to wonder what might have been going on for Ann Hannah at that moment but, while my father seemed not to notice, I have never forgotten her words or the emotion that accompanied them. Thinking about this in my adult years, I could only imagine that the decision to emigrate to Australia happened something like this:

In the years immediately following the First World War, when London was suffering so badly and the emphasis was on rebuilding and getting some semblance of order back into the lives of the

British people, my grandfather just wanted to get away from there and Australia must have seemed like a safe option, far away from the place where the nightmare had occurred. At that same time, Australia was crying out for British families to emigrate, so he went ahead and made enquiries, registered their names and told his wife to prepare for the call-up to be interviewed. Ann Hannah, on the other hand, did not want to leave her home country. Her mother was quite elderly. She had ten brothers and sisters and, while some may have been killed in the war, one can assume that there would still have been a relatively large number of close relatives living in London and surrounds. She grew up there. Her first husband had died there. She gave birth to her four children there and, while it must have been frightening trying to protect three small children and a baby[58] and dealing with the fear created by the new kind of warfare from the air, it was still home. At least one of these bombings hit Ann Hannah's home borough of Shoreditch. It was all she knew, and probably all she wanted. But Arthur had decided otherwise.

It was important to me that my psychological investigation into the depths of Ann Hannah take account of this statement: "I never wanted to come (to this country). 'e made me come." These words signal a sense of displacement, exile and alienation – an experience which, from my reading, is not uncommon among women. Many women throughout the ages, convinced that their husband's work was so much more important than their own, more important too than their family's stability, have been prepared to move to a new place every time their husband was transferred, or decided to take a new job, or just felt like a change. In order to understand the effects of displacement in Ann Hannah's life, I began to research the effects of displacement,

---

58   When the war began in 1914, May was ten, Emily four and Lily, my mother, two. Albert was born in 1915.

dispossession and exile more broadly. Also, I discussed the issue with people who I knew had been in similar situations, in an effort to find out about their particular experiences of displacement.

The personal stories of people who have, historically, been forced to move from their own homes to live in unfamiliar and often unfriendly territory give a clear picture of the effects of displacement. Edward Said, in *Reflections on Exile,* referred to "the crippling sorrow of estrangement." He defined exile as

> the unhealable rift forced between a human being and a native place, between the self and its true home: its essential sadness can never be surmounted.[59]

Mindful of the fact that, at this present time in history, there are millions of people experiencing this "essential sadness" that Said wrote about, displaced from their homes and seeking refuge in other countries, I want to use a broader lens and consider the variety of situations that cause displacement and exile before coming back to a focus on Ann Hannah's particular experience.

Without a doubt, war and conflict heads the list of causes of displacement in these early years of the twenty-first century. In recent memory, the United States, United Kingdom and Australia visited war on the people of Afghanistan and then Iraq. Currently, the President of Syria is at war with his own people causing the displacement of millions of Syrian families. Also, warring groups such as IS (or Daesh), Boko Haram and Al-Qaeda are terrorising, kidnapping, raping and killing people who simply want to go about their own daily lives in peace. Where there is war and conflict, those who are not killed are often forced to flee, resulting in the very visible displacement of individuals, families and communities evident today in many regions of the world.

---

59   Edward Said (2001) *Reflections on Exile and other Literary and Cultural Essays*, p. 137.

According to the United Nations Relief and Work Agency for Palestine Refugees, there are approximately five million Palestinian refugees, 1.4 million of them living in "58 recognised refugee camps in Jordan, Lebanon, the Syrian Arab Republic, the Gaza Strip and the West Bank, including East Jerusalem."[60]

Shahla Abu-Lughod Nakib, a Palestinian woman living in exile, first in Egypt, then the United States and now Amman, Jordan, is one of the literally millions of refugees living in exile around the world. She composed a song to describe her experience of exile:

> I'm a wounded bird
> Living in the world, a stranger ...
> I search, for my country
> But I have nothing but my laments ...[61]

Palestinian people living in East Jerusalem, the West Bank and Gaza are living in occupied territory, dispossessed of their land and way of life. Their homelands are occupied by hundreds of thousands of Israeli settlers who live under Israeli civil law while they themselves are subject to Israel's harsh military law under which "freedom of assembly, freedom of movement, the right to a fair trial, and the right to life are completely suspended."[62]

Neve Gordon, Israeli academic and activist, in his article "From Colonization to Separation: exploring the structure of Israel's occupation," describes the shift in Israeli policy that has deepened and expanded the oppression of Palestinian peoples.

---

60 <http://www.unrwa.org/etemplate.php?id=86>
61 Shahla Abu-Lughod Nakib's song was quoted in an article written by her niece. Lila Abu-Lughod (2012) 'Pushing at the Door: My Father's Political Education, and Mine'. In Penny Johnson and Raja Shehadeh, (Eds.) *Seeking Palestine*, pp. 41–60,
62 <http://punksagainstapartheid.com/the-facts/the-separation-principle/>

The shift, as he explains it, is from the "colonization principle" to the "separation principle:"[63]

> The major difference … between the colonisation and the separation principles is that, under the first principle there is an effort to manage the population and its resources, even though the two are separated. With the adoption of the separation principle Israel loses all interest in the lives of the Palestinian inhabitants and focuses solely on the occupied resources.[64]

Under the separation principle, the occupiers ignore the human-ness of the people they have displaced.

Australia, under its Humanitarian Settlement Scheme, has a history of accepting and assisting refugee families and individuals who apply for refugee status in an orderly fashion. Those desperate enough to risk their lives travelling across the seas in small boats and landing on Australia's shores uninvited and unannounced, however, do not receive the same kind of welcome. In fact, they are treated as criminals and locked up in detention centres for months and, in many instances, for years. To make the point that uninvited asylum seekers will never set foot on the mainland, the Australian government established detention centres on offshore islands such as Christmas Island (Australia), Manus (Papua New Guinea) and Nauru (Nauru).

Conversations I have had with women and men who have come to Australia under the government-approved Humanitarian Settlement Scheme, and who settled in my home town, portray a range of emotions. On the one hand, there is relief for those who

---

63 This discussion is set out more fully in Neve Gordon (2008) *Israeli's Occupation*.

64 Neve Gordon (2008) 'From Colonization to Separation: exploring the structure of Israel's occupation', pp. 25–44. <http://www.tandfonline.com/doi/abs/10.1080/01436590701726442>

have escaped from conflict zones that they no longer have to be in constant fear for their lives and the lives of their children. Similarly, for those who have left situations of hunger and malnutrition, there is relief that they will no longer have to wonder how they will continue to feed themselves and their children. On the other hand, the relief and excitement about the opportunities available to them in a new country are tempered by memories that cannot easily be ignored. For some, there are memories of seeing their parents and other family members murdered, of the fear that engulfed them as they escaped to a neighbouring country, and of the struggle for survival in a refugee camp. For an overwhelming number of women and girls, there are memories of rape, gang rape and other forms of sexual abuse.[65]

In addition to such memories and the need to deal with them, there is for many a constant worry about family members left behind – parents, siblings, even their own children.

The story of Showparaks, recorded in *Our Unspoken Stories: The Stories of Butterflies*, is the story of one woman's struggle to deal with painful memories, including forced separation from her baby daughter. Showparaks fled from Afghanistan to Pakistan with her son and five sisters, from where she and her son were eventually sponsored by a church to go to Canada and begin a new life. After a while, she joined a program run by the Sexual Assault Support Centre of Ottawa (SASC) called The Women, War, Rape and Torture Program (commonly known as Women and War Program) which encouraged women to tell their stories and express the pain that they held deep inside them. In the collection *Our Unspoken Stories*, Showparaks begins her story with the words:

---

65 Eileen Pittaway and Linda Bartolomei (2001) 'Refugees, Race and Gender: The Multiple Discrimination against Refugee Women', pp. 21–32.

> My name is Showparaks (Butterflies). I am in Canada now, but I
> cannot forget a single moment of my past. I live with my memories
> as if they are unfolding over and over again every minute of my days
> … Every moment is so vivid and so real …[66]

As a child, she lived in a small village near Kabul with her parents,
five sisters and two brothers. The two brothers (the youngest of
the children) slept in the same room as their parents, while the
six girls shared a room in another part of the house. One night
when Showparaks was ten years old, she was awoken by a huge
bang. The house was on fire and the room where her parents
and brothers slept was totally destroyed. She carries with her the
memory of the smell of burning flesh and the sight of body parts
strewn around what was left of her house.

The girls continued living in the remains of the house and
survived with the help of neighbours and an uncle. When
Showparaks was fourteen, her uncle arranged her marriage to a
30-year-old man. During her pregnancy with her second child,
her husband was arrested and killed by the religious regime. Then,
on the birth of her second baby, her husband's parents applied for,
and were granted, custody of her two children. They eventually
gave her back her son because he had become too difficult for
them to handle, but refused to return her baby daughter.

When she fled to the refugee camp in Pakistan, she had to
leave without her daughter:

> I had no choice. I had to leave my daughter behind; she was in the
> care of her grandparents. On my way to Pakistan I cried tears that
> I had held back for so long. I cried for the loss of my mother, my
> father, my brothers, my husband, and for all the people who had
> died because of the violence. However, I was crying … yelling …

---

66   Roya Ghafari and Blanca Lopez (2009) *Our Unspoken Stories: The Stories
of Butterflies*, pp. 6–7.

screaming for my daughter, because even though she was still alive, I would not see her again.[67]

Once in Canada, Showparaks fought to have her daughter with her. It took a few years of frustration and depression but the story has a happy ending. Finally, her daughter was granted permission to join her mother in Canada and now mother, son and daughter are making a life together in Ottawa.

In Australia, some of the men and women who have been settled under the Humanitarian Settlement Scheme have expressed their absolute relief and delight at being in a country where they can live free from the horror of the violent conflict which once threatened their lives on a daily basis. Together with the positive effects of resettlement, though, many people who have sought refuge in Australia express profound grief over the loss of familiar lands, and frustration at having to learn a new language and new customs. Many grapple with depression that is the result of persistent memories of fear of violence as well as of actual violence to themselves and their loved ones, but most seem able to accept that such memories will remain a part of their lives as they move forward with determination to establish themselves in their new home.

The experience of migrants, while similar to that of refugees in terms of displacement, is nevertheless different in many respects. A great number of people living in countries around the world are migrants or descendants of migrants. In Australia, for example, all non-Indigenous people are immigrants or descendants of immigrants. From the time when Britain claimed Australia as its own in 1788 and began establishing it as a British colony, convicts were transported from the United Kingdom to work on government infrastructure projects aimed at creating a viable

---

67 *Ibid,* p. 11.

colony. The First Fleet consisted of eleven ships holding over a thousand people including, according to records, 778 convicts – 192 women and 586 men. [68]

Over the years, more and more people came and settled in this young country at the bottom of the earth. Some, like Ann Hannah, came under duress because their husbands had made the decision on behalf of the whole family, leaving them with little choice, while others came willingly with the aim of seeking out new opportunities for themselves and their children. Whether people migrated willingly or under duress, they all would have experienced a sense of displacement, albeit to varying degrees.

The depth of feeling attached to the sense of displacement that migrants experience usually depends on whether or not their migration was voluntary or involuntary. Those who make the choice to migrate in search of better economic and social opportunities, while normally experiencing a degree of displacement, are nevertheless buoyed by the knowledge that they are doing what they chose to do. Even when the reality does not quite measure up to the fantasy, it seems that they find ways of justifying their decision to themselves. Those whose migration was not of their own choosing, on the other hand, often experience a deep sense of displacement compounded by feelings of grief, loss, powerlessness and resentment. While most (both voluntary and involuntary) learn to adjust to their new situation and go on to live productive lives, my discussions with people in such circumstances confirm for me that Edward Said's words do describe the experience of many involuntary migrants: their "essential sadness can never be surmounted."[69]

---

68 Rosalind Miles (2001) *Who Cooked the Last Supper: The Women's History of the World.*

69 Said, p. 137.

For Ukrainian-born Wolodymyr, the decision to migrate to Australia was made in the hope of escaping the trauma of war and the experience of life as a refugee. As is the nature of trauma, however, one cannot escape it by ignoring it. Traumatic events of the past must be faced up to, talked about in all their painful detail and emotions expressed until the events no longer have psychological control over the victim. Revisiting the events and facing one's past squarely and honestly actually frees one up to take back control, but of course for many who are displaced by traumatic events, such memories are extremely hard to face.

Wolodymyr experienced large-scale displacement and trauma twice in his life: once when he was abducted from his native Ukraine by the Germans in 1939 and taken to work in the coal mines of the Ruhr district, and again when he and his German-born wife made the decision to migrate to Australia in 1949.

His daughter, Chris, has written about her father's experiences in an attempt to make sense of her relationship with him. She wrote: "I have never had a meaningful or satisfactory conversation with my father. Even the facts written here had to be laboriously dragged out of him."[70] As Chris tells it, Wolodymyr's first experience of exile happened like this:

> … my father, a simple village lad, was trucked off to Germany. He would never see his family or his homeland again. Working in the coal mines was a dirty, hungry job with punishingly long hours. Each worker was assigned a large volume of coal to dig out and if they didn't reach the quota they just spent the night underground until they did. My father has not talked much about the conditions. He doesn't talk much about any of the trauma he went through. He is too damaged by the experience.[71]

---

70   Personal communication with Betty McLellan, 12 April 2012.
71   *Ibid.*

Eventually, Wolodymyr escaped and made his way to Berlin where he worked for a while in a factory before teaming up with a small group of Ukrainian refugees to walk west to the American zone, where he continued to live in fear of deportation. Trying to understand her father's experience, Chris asks:

> What have been the consequences of his enslavement to the German war machine? He was effectively exiled from home and a family… In village peasant life family is the source of all security and emotional nourishment. To live without family is a kind of living death. My father never even knew whether his mother was still alive after the war. By the time I established contact she was long dead. She never knew if he had survived. He must feel guilt at his abandonment of her.[72]

In 1949, Wolodymyr migrated to Australia. Chris writes:

> So my father escaped by migrating to Australia and left all this trauma behind him. Or did he? I don't think so. I grew up with a brooding silence. My father was hidden behind a wall of ice that he could never afford to melt. Below it is a lava river of hot tears that he will never let himself cry.[73]

In spite of all the negative experiences he had endured, however, his daughter remembers him during her childhood years as "a devoted family man who worked in a secure job for the railways and grew beautiful vegetables".[74]

Echoing the experience of the descendants of Aboriginal Australians who were stolen as children from their families, described by Judy Atkinson as "transgenerational trauma,"[75] Chris describes her own experience of transgenerational trauma.

---

72 *Ibid.*
73 *Ibid.*
74 *Ibid.*
75 Judy Atkinson (2002) *Trauma Trails, Recreating Song Lines: The Transgenerational Effects of Trauma in Indigenous Australia.*

Of her father's seeming lack of outward emotional response, she says:

> I doubt he has cried one tear for his lost homeland, for his lost family, for the trauma of being bombed unmercifully, for being forced to work in intolerable conditions in a foreign country.[76]

Then she goes on to say:

> Instead it is I who have cried the tears. All my life I have cried and cried at the slightest provocation. Only recently I realised that this is no personality defect of mine. I am crying the tears of a deep grief and loss that he has never and will never cry. Growing up around this deeply damaged man I psychically absorbed the trauma. I took on the responsibility of expressing the emotions which were brutalised out of my father. This has crippled my life too, and luckily I have no children to pass this cruel legacy on to.[77]

The example of Philippines-born Nur-isna is quite different from that of Wolodymyr but her feelings of displacement were just as strong. She married a man from a European country and, together, they decided to migrate to a third country, Australia, to settle. Even though Nur-isna participated willingly in the decision to migrate in 1987 with a man she loved and wanted to be with, she experienced serious homesickness. She was the youngest child in a large family and had not anticipated the extent to which she would miss family and friends. Also, she missed her work and the financial independence she had always taken for granted. In Australia, when her husband was at work, she was extremely lonely and frightened, with not even a neighbour to talk to. She explained:

> It was difficult for me that I had to depend on my husband financially and rely on him for everything. I did not have any friends. I also missed celebrating our cultural and religious events with my family. I found the Australian way of life very different from our way of

---

76 Personal communication with Betty McLellan, 12 April 2012.
77 *Ibid.*

living. Our values and beliefs were different. At times I felt like I did not belong here. I was always scared.[78]

As I write these stories, so generously shared with me by Wolodymyr's daughter and by Nur-isna herself, I find myself wondering how Ann Hannah would respond if she were able to read them. I imagine that she would empathise with the feelings of displacement expressed by both of them and, in particular, with the fact that Wolodymyr, once taken from his home village, never saw his mother again. In fact, I can imagine her saying quietly (in a comment aimed at herself as much as at Wolodymyr): "poor bugger."

The reason my siblings and I know so little of our grandmother's early life in London is because she would never talk about it. There were times when one or more of us would ask questions, but we were always met with very brief responses that painted no actual picture that we could hold on to. I always knew that she felt the separation from her mother and siblings very keenly, and that she came to Australia only because her husband forced her to come, but her 'stiff-upper-lip' attitude to life meant that she never allowed herself to dwell on it.

Since white settlement, successive Australian governments have urged people from other countries to consider migrating to Australia for the purposes of boosting the country's population, increasing its economic competitiveness, improving its standard of living and enriching its cultural diversity. At first, with the very racist White Australia Policy in place, only white migrants were accepted. They came in great numbers mainly from the United Kingdom, Italy and Greece and quickly established themselves as productive and loyal Australian citizens. Similarly, when Australia opened its doors to people from Asian, African, Pacific Island and

---

78   *Ibid.*

Middle Eastern countries they too were quick to settle and make their contribution as productive and committed Australians. A government's obsession with promoting the positive aspects of migration, however, often means refusal to shine a light on the negative. Questions arise: How do migrants, men and women, deal with feelings of displacement? Why do so many mature-aged migrant women coming from countries where English is not their first language, keep themselves cloistered in their homes with little or no attempt to learn the language or to engage in life and work outside the home? How many struggle with depression caused by repressed anger at having had migration foisted on them?

I imagine that most women, when faced with the choice of standing their ground and watching their family disintegrate, or going along with their spouse's decision to migrate to a foreign country and keeping their family together, will invariably choose the latter. But for anyone who is forced into such a situation, the sense of displacement and exile can be extreme.

In my discussions with a range of people, I looked for examples of displacement of migrants from one country to another and, also, displacement within a person's own country – internal displacement. Ann Hannah's experience of displacement was from England to Australia. Born and raised with simple working-class values, she went to school for a few years, left school as soon as she was able to and found employment in a laundry where she continued to work during her pregnancies and after her babies were born. She was a simple person who, whether through circumstances or choice, wanted nothing more than a peaceful life, good relationships and enough money and food to sustain her family.

While I am sure she would not have questioned the accepted societal view that men were dominant and women subservient, I have no doubt that she would have had a keen awareness of matters of justice within her marital relationship. I form this opinion mainly from the memories I have of her usual interactions with others and her strict commitment to fairness when adjudicating conflicts between her grandchildren.

I had no knowledge of the kind of relationship my grand-mother had with her first husband until my sister, Bev, told me of the conversation in which Nana called James "the only man she ever loved." Before that, I used to imagine, on the one hand, that he was the love of her life who was tragically taken from her after only a few years of marriage. I imagined that his terminal illness showed itself soon after they married and that Ann Hannah looked after him, heart-broken, until the day he died. On the other hand, I would remind myself that it was just as likely to have been a marriage that was forced on both of them because of pregnancy and the need to establish a home for their daughter Annie May. Indeed, if the UK records are correct, the dates point to that as the more likely scenario. Her marriage to James was on 3 April 1904 and their baby was born on 26 May 1904.

Now that it has been confirmed for me that there *was* love in the relationship, I think it would be right to assume that there would not have been the same degree of inequality and injustice as existed in her marriage to Arthur Stickley. From all accounts, Arthur seems to have been moody, self-focused and destructive in his dealings with his wife and children. His word was law, and my mother and her sisters had interesting stories to tell of the lengths they went to as teenagers in Australia, in collusion with Ann Hannah, to hide their social activities from him. It was convenient for them that he was a heavy drinker and that he fell into a deep sleep quite early most nights. Also, his deafness meant that his sleep was not easily interrupted. As teenagers, they were able to sneak out to dances and other social gatherings with the blessing of their mother and be back long before he woke.

While Ann Hannah and her daughters were able to find ways around his controlling behaviour during those later years, on the matter of migration to Australia in 1921, the decision was entirely his. On his authority as head of the family, he made the arrangements and they could do nothing but acquiesce. Ann Hannah felt the effects of her forced migration keenly. If she had any contact with her mother and siblings once she left England, it had dwindled to nothing by the time I was old enough to think about it. I remember asking about her parents and siblings on one occasion, and she said that she lost touch with them during the war. I presumed she was referring to the Second World War and that she had no idea what happened to any of them during and after that war.

For Ann Hannah, her forced migration did cause a sense of displacement and exile, but it seems that she kept those feelings hidden deep inside her as she got on with her life fully involved in the activities of her family in Australia.

Being forced by one's husband to move from one country to another has been the experience of many women over many decades. For Ann Hannah, it took place in 1921. For other women I have spoken to, it was in the 1950s and 1960s. For some, it continues to occur today and, while the circumstances may be different, the result for women is often very similar.[79]

In the 1950s, Phyllis lived with her husband and family in a small English village until, due to her husband's promotion, the family moved to a large city in South Africa. There they lived for five years before moving back to England. Then, in 1963, the decision was made to move to Australia. With each move, it fell

---

79 Today, it is often the case that women are not 'forced' but, rather, cajoled or even shamed into giving up their own careers and career prospects to support the career ambitions of their partner. Often the decision is a joint one based on the assumption that "if she makes this sacrifice for him now, he will make a similar sacrifice for her later on." The theory is that equality of sacrifice will support equality of success. But the experience of many women is that the second equalising step never eventuates.

to Phyllis to deal with all the practicalities while her husband focused on his work and the opportunities that each move created for him. In addition to all the practical matters, Phyllis also had to contend with her own feelings of displacement, loss of family and friends, loss of familiar territory, and concern about how her children would adjust to a new and unfamiliar culture. With each move, she was aware of the need to integrate into the new country and its customs as quickly as possible.

Looking back on the experiences of displacement, one of Phyllis's children recalled the problems she had as a child and as a teenager. With every move, she said, she experienced anxiety, feelings of inadequacy and, at times, great embarrassment. There were gaps in schooling as she moved from one school to another, and she spoke with a different accent which was the cause of much teasing from other children. The teasing and the embarrassment at being different affected her education in that it resulted in reluctance on her part to speak in class and, to this day, she suffers great anxiety about speaking in public. She felt that, with every move, she struggled to fit in, make friends and feel fully accepted.

A decade later, Elizabeth's experience was similar to that of Phyllis. In the early 1960s, Elizabeth met her future husband while they were both studying at university in New Zealand. They married and had their first child in New Zealand. To further his career, Elizabeth's husband moved with his wife and baby daughter to England so that he could study under an academic whose work was highly respected. From there, they moved to the United States for one year. Then back to England where they moved a couple of times during the six years they were in that country. Then, it was back to the United States. After one year, they moved to a different city within the same state. By that time, there were four children, each of whom held citizenship in a different country.

When Elizabeth's oldest child was fourteen, the family moved to Australia.

Reflecting on fourteen years of instability and feelings of displacement, Elizabeth describes the experience as "very hard."[80] She lost her family of origin when she needed their support the most. Giving birth and bringing up small children on her own was an extremely lonely and sometimes frightening experience. She worked to make new friends with each move but lost those friends when the next move was forced on her, and the cycle started again. With each arrival in a new place, Elizabeth and her children all had to work hard at fitting in and making new contacts.

Elizabeth's oldest daughter reveals that her father had been diagnosed with bipolar disorder ('manic-depression' as it was called at the time) and, her mother seems to have spent all her energy supporting him and his career, to the detriment of her relationship with her children. The daughter identifies the effects of her experience of serial displacement with words like 'solitary', 'anxious', 'embarrassed' at all the taunting by other children, and trying hard to fit in, but never quite making it. Being different, even in other English-speaking countries, she says, attracted a lot of bullying and cruelty.

Internal migration presents problems too, even though the effects on partners and children of the phenomenon of migration within one's own country are often overlooked. Historically, it has been assumed that women and children are happy to move every time their husband and father is required, or chooses, to move, but that assumption is now being questioned.

Carol has been married to the same man for almost fifty years. Reflecting on the roller-coaster ride that characterised the

---

80   Personal communication with Betty McLellan, 12 April 2012.

first twenty-one years of her marriage, she admits that it only stopped because she found the strength and courage to say "no." Counting up the moves, she recalls nineteen moves in twenty-one years – all within Australia. For her husband, moving was a great adventure but for Carol, who just wanted a regular and somewhat predictable life, it was always a chore.[81]

Based on what Carol called her husband's 'wild schemes', she and her two children would only just settle in a new place when they would be off again, sometimes to places where the living conditions were very difficult. One example Carol recalled was that of living in a tin shack with a toddler and a baby in a remote area of outback Australia while her husband worked nearby. The constant experience of displacement was very stressful for her.

Carol's daughter, for whom displacement was a natural part of life (from as early as she can remember until she left home at age eighteen), recalls approaching each move with mixed feelings: excitement about new possibilities, but trauma around packing and unpacking, enrolling in new schools, making new friends and so on. Looking back on her teenage years, she recalls a change in her attitude from worrying about herself to worrying about her mother. She felt her mother's stress and found herself trying to make things right for Carol. She wholeheartedly supported her mother's decision (after twenty-one years of displacement and instability) to refuse any further moves.

As Carol puts it, she had had enough of feeling undervalued and powerless. So, with money she had saved up over the years, she put a deposit on a house and informed her husband that she had moved for the last time. He still came up with 'mad schemes' but knew that Carol could no longer be talked into moving. They are still living in that house twenty-five years after Carol bought it and declared her intentions.

81 *Ibid.*

Another cause of internal migration or displacement that seems largely to have escaped the attention of those who study the effects of displacement and exile is that caused by domestic violence. It has been well documented in feminist literature that one of the strategies of power and control used by violent men against their female partners is that of disconnection from family and friends. The perpetrator's aim is to strip his partner of all means of support by forcing a separation between her and anyone who may have the potential to give her the strength and insight needed to resist him. In such situations of forced disconnection, with no input apart from their partner's criticism and belittling of them, women fairly quickly lose their own identity. Speaking directly to victims of forced isolation, Lundy Bancroft explains that the perpetrator's aim is to "narrow your world," to isolate you so that "his voice is the only voice you hear".[82]

In 1980, scholar and social activist Ellen Pence[83] co-founded the Duluth Domestic Violence Abuse Intervention Project in the United States, and introduced what has come to be known as the 'Power and Control Wheel'. The diagram in the shape of a wheel sets out clearly the pattern of violent and controlling behaviour identified by various researchers. The section headed "Using Isolation" describes the perpetrator's behaviour as controlling what she does, who she sees, who she talks to, what she reads, where she goes; limiting her outside involvement; and using jealousy to justify actions.[84]

The end result of the use of 'isolation' (and no doubt the desired effect in the mind of the perpetrator) is usually a lowering

---

82 <http://lundybancroft.blogspot.com.au/2011/10/breaking-isolation.html>

83 Ellen Pence and Michael Paymar (1993) *Education Groups for Men who Batter: The Duluth Model.* Also see Melanie F. Shepard and Ellen L. Pence (1999) *Coordinating Community Responses to Domestic Violence: Lessons from Duluth and Beyond.*

84 <http://www.theduluthmodel.org/pdf/PowerandControl.pdf>

of self-esteem in the victim and an increased dependence on her abuser.

Every year, there are literally thousands of women and children rendered homeless by the need to escape the violence of their husband and father. In Britain, Nina Lakhani, writing for *The Independent,* revealed that there are huge numbers "of women and children being forced out of their homes by violent relationships":

> Almost 19,000 women aged between 15 and 88 sought state help to find emergency housing in 2008–09, showing the previously hidden scale of domestic-violence 'migrants' forced out of their homes. Sixty per cent, or 11,300 victims, found shelter at a women's refuge – many of which are overstretched and facing unprecedented cuts (to their funding).[85]

The study found that the "average distance travelled was twenty miles in search of safety and housing support."

> The research provides an insight into how far and why women are forced to migrate within the UK … Janet Bowstead, a PhD research student at London Met's child and woman abuse studies unit, said: 'Many of the women have tried to use the law to stay put and get rid of the violent partner, but it hasn't worked – they are forced into these journeys because of their perpetrators'.[86]

In Australia, a recent report revealed that there has been a 33% increase in homelessness due to domestic and family violence since research into the issue began in 2011–12. Of the 279,000 people found to be homeless in the 2015–16 survey, "106,000 (38%) sought support due to domestic and family violence."[87]

---

85 Nina Lakhani (12 April 2012) 'Scale of abuse against women revealed', London: *The Independent.*

86 *Ibid.*

87 Australian Institute of Health and Welfare (15 December 2016) 'More receiving homelessness support due to family violence', <http://aihw.gov.au/media-release-detail/?id=60129557836>

Face-to-face and email conversations I have had with a number of women in Australia indicate that there is a great deal of displacement forced on women and children as a result of the need to escape men's violence. One Australian woman, Lucia, explained in an email to me:

> … it's much more than being rendered homeless. When my children and I fled to a place of safety, I had to leave all my support networks behind. I also had to leave my job. So, I found myself in a new place with no emotional support and no employment.[88]

Another woman, Maryann, spoke of the social isolation forced on her as a result of leaving her violent partner. She wrote:

> It's like I am a pariah now. My friends and family avoid me because they either 1) don't understand the debilitating effects of stress I am subjected to by the DV and then the court process, or 2) they find it too threatening to think about in their own relationships, or 3) they think that I have somehow brought this upon myself, so I deserve what I am getting. Just when I need the most support, I find myself completely alone. As if the horrors of what I have experienced are not enough![89]

Maryann works full-time as a teacher which has meant that her son has had to be in full-time day care since he was ten months old. Also, she describes her involvement with the Family Court as a "nightmare", robbing her of time and energy she would otherwise be giving to her son, not to mention the huge financial burden due to legal fees. Summing up her experience of displacement, she concludes by saying:

> But who can I tell about my losses? Losses of family and friends, of time with my baby, missing his milestones, losses of self-esteem, of hope, of happiness and of dreams. No-one. No-one wants to hear about family court. No-one understands it. No-one wants to hear

---

88 Personal communication with Betty McLellan, 16 April 2012.
89 *Ibid.*

about how men can 'work the system' and use it to continue to inflict misery on women. No-one wants to hear about how I will lose my home and my job. And when I do, I will be regarded by the court as unable to provide a stable home environment for my son.[90]

Internal migration due to the need to escape domestic violence is emotionally and often financially costly, but such displacement is invariably necessary in an attempt to secure the safety of the victim and her children.

Picking up on the concept of 'transgenerational trauma' introduced by Indigenous Australian author Judy Atkinson, and referred to earlier, it is important to recognise the deep sense of displacement caused by the colonisation of Indigenous peoples around the world. As foreigners invaded their lands, those who were not killed were pushed back or pushed out and the original inhabitants found themselves powerless to stop the takeover, not only of their lands but also of their culture, their sacred sites and their way of life. In Australia, many Indigenous men and women refer to Australia Day (the day set aside for celebrations to mark the birth of our nation) as Invasion Day. For them, it marks the beginning of a long history of harsh repression and displacement by British settlers:

> Australian Aboriginal peoples constitute a multitude of tribal and cultural groups. Their presence on the Australian continental land mass can be established as going back as far as 60,000 years, and they represent the oldest continuous identified culture of people in the world today.[91]

---

90 *Ibid.*
91 B. Raphael, P. Swan, and N. Martinek (1998) 'Intergenerational Aspects of Trauma for Australian Aboriginal People'. In Yael Danieli (Ed.) *International Handbook of Multigenerational Legacies of Trauma,* pp. 327–339.

Regardless of their status as the oldest culture on earth, Australian Aboriginal tribes were hunted down by settlers arriving from Britain after 1788 and forcibly removed from their homelands. People from different tribes and different family groups were herded together and forced to live on land that was not familiar to them with people who were not their own tribal people.

Judy Atkinson in *Trauma Trails, Recreating Song Lines,* writes about those early days of displacement as a situation from which generations of Aboriginal men and women have never fully recovered. The trauma of displacement has affected generation after generation as a once secure and proud people still struggle to deal with the trauma caused by forced separation from their lands and the cultural genocide that resulted.[92] The attitude of colonisers everywhere is that the colonisers actually own the land they have invaded. The people, the original owners, are of no consequence. Indeed, in the case of the Aboriginal peoples of Australia, the British colonisers referred to the land as *terra nullius*: land of no people. Such an attitude allowed the colonisers to ignore the rights of Australia's first peoples and to treat them as little more than instruments for their use. Men and women were used as slave labour, forced to work for their white masters for little or no pay. Women were used for sex. Children were stolen from their parents, "forcibly separated from their families and communities since the very first days of the European occupation of Australia."[93]

Aboriginal Lawyer, Pat O'Shane, in her 1995 article 'The Psychological Impact of White Colonialism on Aboriginal People',

---

92 Atkinson, especially pp. 23–92.
93 Human Rights and Equal Opportunity Commission (1997) *Bringing them home: Report of the National Inquiry into the Separation of Aboriginal and Torres Strait Islander Children from Their Families*, p. 27.

focuses on what Judy Atkinson refers to as "transgenerational psychic impacts" or trauma "transmitted across generations:"[94]

> The psychological impact of the experiences of dispossession, denigration and degradation are beyond description. They strike at the very core of our sense of being and identity. ... Throughout Aboriginal society in this country are seen what can only be described by anyone's measure as dysfunctional families and communities, whose relationships with each other are very often marked by anger, depression and despair, dissension and divisiveness. The effects are generational.

Speaking of her own family's experience, Atkinson went on to say:

> I recognised all the things that had happened to me through my grand-parents, and their parents; their brothers and sisters whom I had known as a child; through my mother and her siblings; through my cousins and my siblings. I recognised the things that happened to the thousands of other Aboriginal families like our family, and I marvelled that we weren't all stark, raving mad.[95]

The effects of displacement and dispossession were severe and are, to varying degrees, ongoing for individuals and families with Aboriginal heritage. In addition, there are harrowing examples in Australia of the forced removal of entire Aboriginal communities. One example still very fresh in my mind decades on from when I first knew about it is that of the forced removal of the people of Mapoon in North Queensland.

The community of Mapoon was established as a mission by Moravian missionaries on behalf of the Presbyterian Church of Australia on the traditional lands of the Tjungundji people on the Western shores of Cape York Peninsula in 1891.

---

94 Atkinson, p. 81.
95 Pat O'Shane (1995) 'The Psychological Impact of White Colonialism on Aboriginal People', pp. 151–3.

Mark Gillespie, in his article 'Mapoon: the burning of a community' (2008), looks at what he calls "the shameful history of Mapoon – an Aboriginal community declared unviable and burned to the ground forty-five years ago." On the orders of the then Premier of Queensland, Joh Bjelke-Petersen, a terrified people lost everything that had hitherto given meaning to their lives:

> On November 15, 1963, an armed detachment of Queensland Police arrived at the Aboriginal community of Mapoon with orders to forcibly remove 23 Aboriginal residents and to 'commence demolition of the vacated shanties on the Reserve'.
>
> That night the police burst into people's homes and rounded up the occupants. The next day they were hauled off on a barge as their homes and community buildings were burnt to the ground.
>
> 'Yes, I saw them go up in flames' said Mapoon resident Simon Peter. 'From my Mother-In-Law's place down they burnt everything … The Church, cookhouse, school, work-shop, butcher shop, store all burnt down …'
>
> The burning of Mapoon was the culmination of a vicious campaign to remove the Aboriginal residents. The state Coalition government justified this brutal repression arguing it 'was in their own interests and the interest of their children. Mapoon was a hopeless proposition if their children were to succeed as assimilated members of the community'.
>
> The government's assimilationist agenda, however, was never about Aboriginal welfare. The biggest deposit of bauxite in the world and the desire to develop an aluminum industry in Queensland was what drove their policy.[96]

I have a memory that stays with me of an Indigenous elder expressing her deep sadness and disbelief about the destruction of Mapoon at a Women's Conference attended by Indigenous

---

96   Mark Gillespie (2008) 'Mapoon: the burning of a community',
     <http://www.solidarity.net.au/7/mapoon-the-burning-of-a-community/>

and non-Indigenous women in the 1980s. Indigenous leaders had organised a Yarning Circle open only to Indigenous women. Non-Indigenous women were invited to sit around the outside of the circle and observe. During a conversation about harsh and insensitive treatment by politicians, Aunty Jean, a long-time resident of old Mapoon, spoke about the destruction of her community twenty years earlier. As she told her story, simple words were seared on my memory: "They even burnt our church." It was obvious that the distress Aunty Jean felt about the callous way the authorities destroyed her place of worship had not eased with the intervening years – and her distress is something I have never forgotten.

There is no doubt that forced removal of the people of Mapoon was on the Government's agenda, in the event that the people refused to go willingly, when they passed the Comalco Act in 1957. At that time, the bauxite company Comalco was given 8,000 square kilometres of Aboriginal Reserve land by the Government with no provision for compensation for Aboriginal people. Indeed, as Gillespie points out in that same article, the Act "didn't even mention the existence of Aboriginal people."[97]

During that period, from 1957 until the eventual forced removal of the community in 1963, the government and the church (the same church that originally established the Mapoon community) worked together, employing heartless and destructive tactics in an attempt to have the people leave willingly. For example, the church threatened the people with closure of the store, school and medical facilities and painted a picture of a destitute community where the children would be labeled 'neglected' and taken from their parents by the government. Another tactic used against the people was that of separating families. Those who were accused of stirring up trouble were

---

97   Gillespie (2008).

removed. A wife who went to hospital on Thursday Island to have a baby would not be allowed to return because the authorities knew that, if she was prevented from returning, her family would eventually go to be with her.

No matter what tactics the government employed, however, the resistance of the small Mapoon community remained strong, until the day they were forcibly removed by armed police and everything they held dear was burnt to the ground. A whole community of people was dispossessed of its land in a most violent way.

For Indigenous people, any internal migration outside their own lands is usually migration that is forced on them, and causes a sadness and a sense of estrangement that cannot be easily overcome.

Edward Said's definition of exile or displacement as "the unhealable rift forced between a human being and a native place" and his conclusion that "its essential sadness can never be surmounted,"[98] resonates with all of the personal testimonies recorded in this chapter – with refugees, victims of occupation by a more powerful nation or victims of war and conflict; with migrants, especially involuntary migrants forced into lives of displacement by the decisions and actions of others; with women isolated in their own homes or forced from their homes by the violent behaviour of their partners; and with Indigenous peoples and their descendants displaced by colonising forces.

In this context, Ann Hannah's words expressed with such emotion so long ago, make sense: "I never wanted to come (to this country). 'e made me come." Forced by her husband to leave her native England, Said's words suggest that she probably lived the rest of her life with an 'essential sadness' that could

---

98   Said, p. 137.

75

never be surmounted. Regardless of such sadness, however, and in spite of the violence perpetrated against her and her children by her husband, she made a life for herself and her family and demonstrated the kind of resilience that meant that only on very rare occasions did she acknowledge her sense of loss and displacement.

CHAPTER FOUR

"'e was a wickid man" [99]

This is the chapter I have been dreading but, at the same time, it is the one that I am impatient to write because of my belief that the situation discussed here explains more than anything else Ann Hannah's determination to survive and thrive. Exploring this particular saying will, I believe, allow me to understand more fully the pain she must have felt and to gain a clearer picture of her amazing resilience. I cannot hide the fact that there is a kind of excitement in me as I face the possibility of knowing my grandmother in a way that she never allowed anyone to know her in life.

When I first heard Ann Hannah say of her late husband: "'e was a wickid man," it was puzzling to me because, to that point, I had never heard anything about my grandfather that could, in my estimation, be classed as wicked.

Arthur Stickley died a few years before I was born. Hence, I never knew him but I have seen photographs of him: one portrait-type and one with his wife and the four children taken soon after their arrival in Australia. He was a tall man with dark hair and a large moustache. That is the picture I have in my mind

---

99   'Wicked' here is spelled as Ann Hannah pronounced it: wickid.

of his physical appearance. Other snippets of information I have picked up over the years have helped me broaden my picture of him: he was totally deaf; drank a lot; made his own home brew (which Dad used to drink with him when he was courting Mum). He worked as a maintenance man in the laundry where Nana and her three daughters also worked. In the family, he was a bully – violent to Ann Hannah if he didn't get his own way and very strict with the children.

I remember as a child asking Ann Hannah about my grandfather. She obviously found the thought of talking about him very distasteful because all she said was "'e was a wickid man" and that was the end of the conversation. As I recall it now, there was a sad, almost haunting tone in her voice. Was it hatred, regret, helplessness? Pondering on it now as an adult in possession of more facts, I am able to conclude with some confidence that it was probably all three. At the time, however, I really could not see that his sins were as bad as the word 'wicked' implied.

Brewing his own beer hardly qualifies as wicked, I thought. Not letting his daughters go out dancing, being a bully, insisting on his own way in everything, all indicate that he was a thoroughly unlikeable person, but wicked? Then, there was the story about how he tricked Australian immigration officials in England when family members had to front up for various checks to see if they were eligible candidates for emigration to Australia. I could never find out exactly how he did it, but the story goes that, because he was afraid that his severe deafness might make him ineligible, he devised a way to put his family through all the health checks while avoiding any scrutiny of his own health. Pretty clever I thought, and dishonest – but hardly wicked.

It was to be some years before I understood the reason for the hatred and regret and helplessness that I heard in Ann Hannah's voice that day. My grandfather had sexually abused Nana's oldest daughter for many years. Annie May White, our Aunty May, was a victim of sexual abuse at the hands of her stepfather from a very young age, a situation which continued well into her teenage years.[100] In keeping with the times, this terrible family shame was never talked about openly. Whether or not May complained about it to her mother or sisters in private while the abuse was going on, I will never know, but it is clear from subsequent events that they did come to know of it at some stage.

I stumbled on the information about Arthur Stickley's abuse of his stepdaughter one day when I was on a brief visit home as a young adult. My mother's two sisters, May and Em, were visiting our home and I overheard an argument between the three sisters in another room. The argument came to a climax with May screaming: "You'll never know what *your* father did to me." Then, Em's voice (distressed, but devoid of empathy) yelled: "Don't blame us for what our father did. It wasn't our fault." My mother, Lilian (Lil), who was more reserved than her two sisters, didn't say a word, but her silence makes her no less guilty of failure to show empathy. The sisters obviously did know about the abuse but, in their powerlessness, were not able to show May the support she so desperately needed even in their later years.

My grandfather was, indeed, a wicked man. His sexual abuse of his stepdaughter and, as I was to discover years later, the rape of his wife, continued over many years. In accordance with the testimony of other victims of sexual crimes, Ann Hannah would have lived with the consequences of his deeds every day that she was married to him and, in fact, every day of her long life. It is those consequences that I explore here as I continue to develop this psychological biography of my grandmother.

---

100 Annie May's father, Ann Hannah's first husband James White, died when May was only three years old.

The central theme of this chapter is that which is variously referred to as father-daughter rape, father-daughter incest or sexual abuse of children within the home. I refer to it here as father-daughter rape. In exploring this phenomenon, I approached my reading with certain questions in mind. How has psychology dealt with father-daughter rape historically, and how have feminists responded to psychology's treatment of the issues? How prevalent is the practice? Why do perpetrators do it? And, what is society's general attitude toward fathers who rape their children? Only after refreshing my memory about the research on all of these issues did I feel ready to focus on the victims – Annie May and her mother Ann Hannah – and the effects on them of the abuse they endured. In particular, how was Annie May affected at the time and throughout her whole life? And, most pertinent for this psychological biography, how did the prolonged abuse of Annie May by her stepfather affect Ann Hannah, wife of the abuser and mother of the abused?

Most feminist commentary about the way psychology and psychiatry have historically handled the matter of the sexual abuse of girls by their fathers, stepfathers, brothers and grandfathers begins with Sigmund Freud and his spectacular betrayal of victims of this serious crime. This is something I have written about previously,[101] but I will revisit it briefly here. It is interesting that the abuse of Annie May by her stepfather occurred around the same time as Freud made his 'discovery' that such a thing existed only in the fantasies of little girls. How can that be, given that it was actually happening to Annie May? It was real. But Freud declared that fathers would never do such a thing so, in the mind

---

101 Betty McLellan (1995) *Beyond Psychoppression: A Feminist Alternative Therapy*. 1995, pp. 77–81.

of the revered founder of psychoanalysis, it had to be fantasy.[102]

At first, Freud did believe his patients. In 1896, in a letter to his friend Wilhelm Fliess, he expressed concern about the number of women patients who told him similar stories of sexual abuse and he declared that the cause of the anxiety neurosis many of his patients were suffering was not to be found in their minds (not in fantasy) but in actual physical events. Girls were being used by their close male relatives for sexual gratification and the anxiety his patients were experiencing in their teenage and adult years was due to that sexual abuse.[103] So convinced was he that he immediately prepared a series of three papers on 'The Aetiology of Hysteria'[104] outlining his theory that "Hysteria originated in a sexual seduction at an early (prepubescent) age,"[105] and he named the seducers as "close relatives, a father or a brother."[106]

While Freud's analysis was convincing, his colleagues were not persuaded. Their reaction to the suggestion that fathers were molesting their daughters was swift and severe. One by one, they rejected his ideas and he soon found himself isolated within his profession and from the friendship of his peers. Personally devastated by such rejection, Freud went into a period of self-reflection and, to the absolute amazement of feminists and child advocates to this day, he then completely reversed his theory within one year.

Florence Rush in *The Best Kept Secret: Sexual Abuse of Children* discusses the progression of Freud's thinking during that brief period of reflection. She saw from his letters to Fliess that, while

---

102 James Strachey (Tr. and Ed. 24 Vols.) (1953-1974). *Standard Edition of the Complete Psychological Works of Sigmund Freud*. Vol. 1, p. 259.

103 Strachey, Vol. 1, p. 246.

104 Anxiety conditions were, at that time, referred to as hysteria.

105 Jeffrey Masson (1990) *Against Therapy*, p. 87.

106 Charles Bernheimer and Claire Kahane (Eds.) (1985) *In Dora's Case: Freud-Hysteria-Feminism*, p. 13.

he remained "staunch on sexual trauma as the cause of neurosis," he was "extremely unhappy with the idea of father as seducer."[107] In February 1897, he admitted to Fliess that "the number of fathers named by his patients as sexual molesters had truly alarmed him."[108] In May 1897, he describes a dream in which he himself had "affectionate" feelings toward his eleven-year-old daughter Mathilde. Troubled by that dream and by persistent thoughts that his own father may have abused one of Freud's sisters, he quickly closed his mind to such possibilities and declared that fathers would not, in reality, behave in that way. This, according to Rush, marks the beginning of Freud's turn-around on his seduction theory. The stories he had been hearing from so many of his female patients were simply fantasies. Fathers were not guilty of molesting their daughters, he concluded with a degree of relief, but daughters were guilty of indulging in "infantile wish fulfilments, fantasies rather than memories."[109]

In September 1897, Freud explained his turn-around to Fliess:

> I no longer believe in my neurotica ... I shall start at the beginning and tell you the whole story of how the reasons for rejecting it arose. The first group of factors were the continual disappointment of my attempts to bring my analyses to a real conclusion, the running away of people who for a time had seemed my most favourably inclined patients, the lack of the complete success on which I had counted ... Then there was the astonishing thing that in every case ... blame was laid on perverse acts by the father ... though it was hardly credible that prevented [sic] acts against children were so general ... Thirdly, there was the definite realization that there is no

---

107 Florence Rush (1980) *The Best Kept Secret: Sexual Abuse of Children*, pp. 88–89.
108 *Ibid,* pp. 90–91.
109 Bernheimer and Kahane, p. 14.

'indication of reality' in the unconscious, so that it is impossible to distinguish between truth and emotionally-charged fiction.[110]

Conveniently locating his patients' testimonies in the unconscious where there is no "indication of reality" allowed Freud then to develop his Oedipus theory which postulates that boys have unconscious sexual longing for their mothers and girls for their fathers. Elizabeth Ward, in *Father-Daughter Rape*, suggests that the Oedipus theory was a convenient explanation for father-daughter rape:

> This device enabled him to turn ... concrete reality ... into the theory of a fantasy wish for sexual pleasure with the father (i.e. men). We still see the effects every day: 'You're making it up!' – an especially common response to girl-children who complain of sexual assault.[111]

Hence, generations of psychologists and psychiatrists have distrusted the stories of countless numbers of girls and women, and enabled perpetrators to continue their abuse with impunity. Judith Herman refers to it as Freud's legacy:

> The legacy of Freud's inquiry into the subject of incest was a tenacious prejudice, still shared by professionals and laymen alike, that children lie about sexual abuse. This belief is by now so deeply ingrained in the culture that children who dare to report sexual assault are more than likely to have their complaints dismissed as fantasy.[112]

Louise Armstrong suggested that "Freud's colleagues and compatriots breathed a collective sigh of relief" at the finding that "the girl's shame and disgust were due not to the actual violation, but to a girl's deep, unconscious wish for her father, her

---

110 Rush, p. 92.
111 Elizabeth Ward (1984) *Father-Daughter Rape*, p. 107.
112 Judith Herman (1981) *Father-Daughter Incest*. p. 11.

fantasies."[113] From then on, Freud's disciples set about refining this new theory that then became enshrined in psychological lore as the only way to assess and respond to testimonies from victims of father-daughter rape.

This is the context in which Annie May's abuse by her stepfather occurred. I am not suggesting that Freud's original discovery or his subsequent cover-up would have had any direct influence on the case of Annie May, but it does speak volumes about the entrenched attitudes of people in general, and professionals in particular, toward this 'invisible' crime at that time. May was born in 1904 and, from bits of information I have been able to glean, the abuse started around 1911 when she was seven years old. Freud and his disciples were at that very time continuing to influence attitudes throughout Europe based on the false premise that fathers were innocent and daughters guilty of fantasy. In 1921, Ann Hannah's family migrated to Australia where Arthur Stickley's abuse of his stepdaughter continued until May was about eighteen years old.

Most reports on child sexual abuse include comments about prevalence. How prevalent is the practice? A massive study undertaken by the World Health Organisation in 2002 into the health effects of all types of violence, begins the section on sexual abuse by stating that "[e]stimates of the prevalence of sexual abuse vary greatly depending on the definitions used and the way in which information is collected." Studies of adults reporting on their own childhood sexual abuse, they found, varied from 1% to 19% for men and 0.9% to 45% for women.[114] Prevalence varied, also, from country to country.

---

113 Louise Armstrong (1994) *Rocking the Cradle of Sexual Politics,* p. 16.
114 World Health Organization (2002) *World Report on Violence and Health,* pp. 63–4.

In an article written in 1984 for the *New Internationalist*, using the word 'incest' to include "all cases of sexual assault by a trusted adult familiar to the victim," Debbie Taylor maintains that incest "is a truly worldwide phenomenon" and occurs in one in four families:

> Everywhere studies have been done the evidence is the same. And in the overwhelming majority of cases (80–90 per cent) it is girl-children that are the victims: sexually abused by fathers, uncles, grandfathers, brothers, fathers-in-law, neighbours, family friends. In Cairo a survey in 1973 found between 33 and 45 per cent of families contained daughters who had been raped, molested, 'interfered with' by a relative or close family friend. Kinsey's 1953 study in the US found incest in 24 per cent of families. And the figures are similar in the UK and Australia.[115]

In 1997, J. Fleming conducted a study in Australia using 710 randomly selected women and found that 144 (20%) had been victims of sexual abuse as children.[116]

In an attempt to expose what Florence Rush called "the best kept secret", feminists writing in the 1970s, 1980s and 1990s drew attention to the prevalence of the sexual abuse of children. Calling it "a common occurrence", Judith Herman said: "Female children are regularly subjected to sexual assaults by adult males who are part of their intimate social world."[117] Referring to Florence Rush's "long dark Age of Permitted Abuse," Louise Armstrong added that fathers "wielded absolute power over their children's lives ... Within a total patriarchal structure, sexual use

---

115 Debbie Taylor (5 August 1984) 'Kiss Daddy Goodnight', in *New Internationalist*, 138, <http://newint.org/features/1984/08/05/kiss/>

116 J.L. Fleming (1997) 'Prevalence of childhood sexual abuse in a community sample of Australian women', pp. 65–68, <http://europepmc.org/abstract/med/9033559>

117 Herman, p. 7.

of children was permitted and presumed."[118] Elizabeth Ward introduced her report of the findings of her Australian research by saying

> The more I read, and the more that women talked to me about their experiences, the more it became clear to me that ... I was looking ... at a phenomenon of epic proportions ... I found an enormous proportion of girl-children raped, molested, abused and used by their father, stepfather, de facto father, grandfather, uncle, brother...[119]

More recently, the American Academy of Child and Adolescent Psychiatry began a report on the prevalence of child sexual abuse in the United States with the words:

> Child sexual abuse has been reported up to 80,000 times a year, but the number of unreported instances is far greater, because the children are afraid to tell anyone what has happened, and the legal procedure for validating an episode is difficult.[120]

From all of the reports quoted here, it is clear that the sexual abuse of children continues unabated. It seems that it is no less prevalent today (and no less tragic) than it was when Annie May was being abused by her stepfather in the early years of the twentieth century.

The question often asked by women and men struggling to understand the agenda of perpetrators is "Why do they do it?" A quick answer is, "Because they can!" Children are such easy prey. Men who forego any thought of the effect their predatory behaviour will have on their victims and the lifelong damage

---

118 Armstrong, p. 14.
119 Ward, p. 3.
120 American Academy of Child and Adolescent Psychiatry (2011), <http://www.aacap.org/cs/root/facts_for_families/child_sexual_abuse>

that their actions will cause, choose instead the path of instant gratification – sexual gratification and, more particularly, gratification of their need for power and control. To quote Erikson again, the first psychosocial lesson children learn in life is that of "trust"[121] and, having learnt that lesson, their instinct is to trust adults. Those adults who sexually abuse children betray that trust and, in so doing, rob their victim/s of any chance of a normal healthy childhood.

Studies reveal that victims of childhood sexual abuse by priests, teachers and other leaders in a variety of community organisations are both boys and girls but that, within the home, it is overwhelmingly girls who are targeted.

In Australia in 2012, Prime Minister Julia Gillard announced that she would be recommending to the Governor General that a Royal Commission into Institutional Responses to Child Sexual Abuse be conducted. Then, on 11 January 2013, Governor General Quentin Bryce appointed six commissioners and directed them to "inquire into institutional responses to allegations and incidents of child sexual abuse and related matters ..." Initially, the federal government requested that the final report be submitted by 31 December 2015, but the number of submissions, interviews and written reports by victims was so great that the date for the submission of the final report was extended to 15 December 2017. There is no doubt that this particular Royal Commission has been and continues to be a valuable tool. It not only allows for the naming of perpetrators but, also, provides a situation where victims are finally heard – and believed. The sense of relief expressed by individual victims and the sense that justice is finally being done is overwhelmingly healing for individuals and for the Australian community as a whole.

---

121 Erikson, pp. 57–66.

The question now on the lips of victims of child sexual abuse *in the home* is "When will justice be pursued for me?" Admittedly, it would be much more difficult for the federal government to conduct a royal commission into child sexual abuse in the home but it would not be impossible. Women victims of child sexual abuse by fathers, stepfathers, brothers, grandfathers and 'friends' of the family stand ready to respond.

If Aunty May had had the opportunity to tell her story to a Royal Commission, I wonder if she would have taken up the opportunity. Yes, I think she would have because, even though she suffered the effects of having been abused for so long, she was a fighter in her own way. I imagine that she would have seen such an opportunity as a way of achieving some kind of justice, and would have taken it.

Why do 'wickid' men perpetrate such abuse and misery on their victims? What is their agenda? Some say it is simply to satisfy their own sexual urges. Indeed, that seemed to be Ann Hannah's opinion in relation to her husband's abuse of Annie May. I'm indebted to my younger sister Beverley for information that I had not been privy to. When we three older siblings had left home and Bev was still living at home while she continued her nursing training, Mum occasionally talked to her about these things. She recalls our mother saying that there were often terrible rows between her parents about sex and that "if Nana didn't come good" he would go to Aunty May. Consequently, according to our mother, Nana would most often give in so that his 'sex needs' would be satisfied.

In today's terms, this is clearly marital rape, though Ann Hannah would not have seen it that way. There was, at that time, a general belief in society, backed up by the law, that women could not be raped by their spouses due to the fact that women became 'men's property' on their wedding day. Indeed, such a belief was so entrenched that feminists in Australia were not able to force a change in the law until the 1980s.[122] During all the years that Ann Hannah was being raped by her husband, he – and she – would have interpreted it as his right.

I remember a conversation I had with my mother when I was a young adult in which she revealed that a good friend of hers was "at the end of her tether" because her husband wanted sex all the time – every morning, every evening and, when he could get away from work, even at lunchtime. When I expressed my horror, Mum's response was that "some women are unlucky with the husband they end up with." The attitude at that time was that the man had a right to do as he liked and that the woman was either 'lucky' or 'unlucky'. In those terms, Ann Hannah was very unlucky indeed. Knowing that her only option was to put up with her own abuse, Ann Hannah seems to have decided that giving into her husband for sex would be one way to minimise his abuse of Annie May. However, the belief that the sexual abuse of children is primarily about the sex needs of the abuser is a common misconception. As countless studies reveal, the agenda of perpetrators is overwhelmingly a need for power and control, rather than for sex.

The website of the Domestic Violence Resource Centre Victoria states very clearly:

> The reason men sexually abuse children is connected to their need to feel powerful and in control. It is not about sex. He is in control of his behaviour and can choose not to abuse.[123]

The Australian Institute of Family Studies (AIFS) Research Report, 'Insights into sexual assault perpetration', also confirms the centrality of power and control as motives:

---

122 Patricia Easteal (1998) 'Rape in Marriage: Has the Licence Lapsed?
      In P. Easteal (Ed.). *Balancing the Scales: Rape, Law Reform and Australian Culture*, pp. 107–123.
123 <http://www.dvrcv.org.au/help-advice/sexual-abuse-in-childhood>

In the victim/survivors' accounts, control, power and domination emerge as central but complex aspects of perpetration. Having control over the victim/survivor was a clear resource for perpetrators.[124]

The authors of that report, Haley Clark and Antonia Quadara, also quote the work of J. Jordan:

> The act of rape involves not only the physical violation of another body, but an attempt to secure total control and dominance. What many rapists are seeking is a sense of their own power, their ability to subordinate another to their will.
>
> Sensing fear in their victims can serve as an aphrodisiac, an indication that their mastery of the situation is being achieved. Most rapists need no other weapon to secure victim compliance.[125]

Arthur Stickley's ongoing rape of both his wife and stepdaughter must have given him a feeling of power and mastery that was not available to him in any other aspect of his life. For a time, I wondered if he had abused his stepdaughter so consistently because she was not his own child, a kind of punishment for being another man's daughter. Maybe he felt justified in humiliating and using her because he saw her as an 'intruder' in his home, I thought. But a conversation I had with Emily, the middle sister between Aunty May and my mother, put an end to such musings. A few years after Mum and Aunty May had died, I plucked up the courage to ask Aunty Em, "Did the old boy abuse you and Mum like he did Aunty May?" She responded, "Me, a bit. But nothing like he did to May." I could barely get my next question out because, if my own mother had suffered such abuse and I hadn't at least attempted to let her talk about it, I didn't really want to

---

124 Haley Clark & Antonia Quadara (2010) *Insights into Sexual Assault Perpetration: Giving Voice to Victim/Survivors' Knowledge*.

125 J. Jordan (2008) *Serial survivors: Women's Narratives of Surviving Rape*, p. 6.

know. I asked "What about Mum?" Aunty Em's reply came with a somewhat cynical tone: "Oh no. She was the pet. Nothing bad ever happened to her." I felt sad for May and Em, but very relieved to know that, at least according to Aunty Em's account, my own mother had not been forced to live with the ongoing trauma that almost always follows sexual abuse in childhood.

It seems, then, that Arthur Stickley's agenda was probably not to satisfy his sexual urges nor to punish Annie May for being an 'intruder' in his home but, rather, it was primarily an attempt to have power and control over her – and, it naturally follows, over her mother Ann Hannah and the whole family. A wicked man, indeed.

As I continued my study, I was interested to read articles that discussed society's general response to child sexual abuse. I knew that the majority of women and men in societies where the healthy development of children is valued would never sanction sexual grooming, sexual approaches, sexual activity by adults toward children. It is accepted, intuitively, that such behaviour is damaging to children. But when children *are* being sexually abused by adults, many in society seem unable to deal with the situation. Whether it is abuse by priests and other leaders in the community, or abuse in the home, the response from society has historically been less than satisfying.

Many people prefer to pretend the abuse isn't happening. When the suspected abuser is a high profile entertainer, a sports coach, a priest or other leader, some question their own right to accuse such powerful men and many have, in the past, opted for the safer route of convincing themselves that they are probably imagining it. When it is a father or other family member, many still believe that they do not have the right to comment on what may or may not be happening inside someone else's family. Pretending that the sexual abuse of a child is not happening when it clearly is has meant that countless numbers of children have suffered many more years of abuse than they needed to.

Another attitude prevalent in society is that the victim must be lying. It seems that it is much easier to blame the victim, as Sigmund Freud did, than to confront the awful fact that a great number of men in societies around the world are prepared to exploit a child, with no thought for the wellbeing of that child.

Closely related to the belief that child sexual abuse victims are lying is the need many people seem to have to find ways to excuse perpetrators. It is for this reason that they can continue to abuse with impunity. Many victims keep the abuse secret because they feel somehow to blame for the abuse and are sure that their mothers would be angry with them if they found out. However, even when a child does tell and is believed, many people are desperate to find excuses for the perpetrator's behaviour. On those rare occasions when the police are involved and a charge of sexual abuse of a minor is laid, it is an extremely difficult charge to prove and, consequently, very few perpetrators are found guilty in the courts. When a perpetrator *is* found guilty, the punishment imposed often reflects society's unwillingness to believe men capable of this kind of destructive behaviour toward children and a readiness to look for excuses. Defence lawyers who focus on 'mitigating circumstances' such as alcoholism, mental illness or stress about the break-up of a relationship, usually find a jury and a society only too eager to accept such explanations. In all, perpetrators have little reason to fear society's sanctions for this crime.

More than a hundred years ago, when men were free to do as they liked in their own home with their own families, those who chose to perpetrate abuse did so with impunity. Ann Hannah and Annie May had no protection under the law, a situation that Arthur Stickley exploited mercilessly, to the detriment of his whole family.

In line with reports about the effects of child sexual abuse, it is reasonable to assume that the victims of Arthur Stickley's abuse suffered lifelong effects – his stepdaughter Annie May, his wife Ann Hannah, his daughter Emily and, by extension, his other children Lilian and Albert. In order to achieve a greater understanding of my grandmother, I sought to refresh my memory about the studies undertaken into the effects of child sexual abuse on victims and on mothers of victims.

Important research undertaken in 1985 by David Finkelhor and Angela Browne listed "fear, anxiety, depression, anger and hostility, aggression, and sexually inappropriate behavior" as among the initial effects on child victims. The list of long-term effects included "depression and self-destructive behavior, anxiety, feelings of isolation and stigma, poor self-esteem."[126]

In an article 'The Effects of Sexual Abuse' (2000), the Jordan Institute for Families (North Carolina Division of Social Services) wrote:

> The impact of sexual abuse on children can be devastating and long-lasting. Because children are victimized by someone they should be able to trust and depend on, they may not realize that the abuse is wrong and not their fault ... [S]exually-abused children report feeling that something is wrong with them, that the abuse is their fault, and that they should blame themselves for the abuse.[127]

The American Academy of Child and Adolescent Psychiatry (AACAP) stated in the first paragraph of a report on child sexual abuse: "The long-term emotional and psychological damage of sexual abuse can be devastating to the child." The researchers went

---

126 David Finkelhor and Angela Browne (October 1985) 'The Traumatic Impact of Child Sexual Abuse: A Conceptualization'. pp. 530–541.
127 Jordan Institute for Families (June 2000) 'The Effects of Sexual Abuse', <http://www.practicenotes.org/vol5_no2/effects_of_sexual_abuse.htm>

on to describe the stress, anxiety and confusion children suffer because of the abuse:

> The child of five or older who knows and cares for the abuser becomes trapped between affection or loyalty for the person, and the sense that the sexual activities are terribly wrong. If the child tries to break away from the sexual relationship, the abuser may threaten the child with violence or loss of love. When sexual abuse occurs within the family, the child may fear the anger, jealousy or shame of other family members, or be afraid the family will break up if the secret is told.[128]

From information I picked up over many years, the effects suffered by Annie May seem to have included depression, anxiety, PTSD, sleep problems, low self-esteem and (at times) feelings of worthlessness. Also, remembering the closeness of my mother and Emily and comparing it with the slightly more distant relationship they both had with May, it could be that she experienced a sense of isolation, a feeling that she was 'different' from her two sisters. The most vivid memory I have of Aunty May's general health is that she suffered seriously high blood pressure and unbearable headaches much of the time.

It was only when Annie May began dating at around age eighteen that her stepfather's abuse stopped. Eventually, she met Jack who, according to reports from my mother, was very protective of May right from the start of their relationship. May and Jack married and had two children, my cousins Patricia (Pat) and Neville. As a family, they seemed happy. What a relief it must have been for May finally to experience a 'normal' life. Sadly, May's normal, happy relationship was cut short when the

---

128 American Academy of Child and Adolescent Psychiatry (November 2014) 'Child Sexual Abuse', <https://www.aacap.org/AACAP/Families_and_Youth/Facts_for_Families/FFF-Guide/Child-Sexual-Abuse-009.aspx>

children were young teenagers. Jack, who worked as a delivery driver, was involved in a car accident one day at work and died instantly. Even though I was only in my early teens, I still have a clear memory of Aunty May's inconsolable grief.

After that, she showed no sign of wanting to marry again. She struggled single-handedly through her children's teenage years, was happy with their choice of partners and enjoyed a warm relationship with her grandchildren.

Outside the home, my predominant memory of Aunty May is her involvement with the Order of the Eastern Star which, at that time, I saw as a kind of service club for women. They had rituals and office-bearers and seemed to be committed to raising money for medical research and providing other services for disadvantaged groups. Information I gleaned as I grew older was that the Order of the Eastern Star is an international organisation closely related to the Masons. In fact, when the Order was established, a woman seeking to join had to be related in some way to a Mason – wife, widow, daughter, sister, mother. That rule was subsequently relaxed and other women 'of good standing' (like Aunty May) were accepted as members. In her local Chapter, May rose to the top and served for a year as Associate Matron followed by the pinnacle position, Worthy Matron. She was rightly proud of her success in the Order and seemed to enjoy the friendship of the other members.

May lived a long and productive life, in spite of the abuse she suffered throughout her childhood, and died at the age of 89.

While I realise that the actual target of child sexual abuse, the child, must remain at the centre of concern in psychological and sociological research, the other person deserving of attention and concern is the mother of the victim. Feminist researchers and writers have drawn attention to the fact that, since patriarchal societies around the world have so much invested in presenting men in an acceptable light, women and children are often targeted for blame. In the case of child sexual abuse, when the secret is uncovered, society seems to go into overdrive in an effort to 'excuse' the perpetrator. In some instances, the child victim is blamed. "She always acted in a sexual way around her father." "She teased him, led him on." "She could have said 'no' but didn't." Such accusations, apart from the ludicrous image of a grown man coming under the spell of a seven-year-old, ignore the fact that sexual abuse of a child by an adult is, in every case, a decision that the adult makes.

More prevalent than blaming the child victim, however, is blaming the victim's mother. Since the 1960s, 'mother-blaming' has been the subject of much research and writing by feminists and non-feminists alike. In every generation, the same accusations have been directed at mothers: "If she had been satisfying his sex needs, he wouldn't have had to look elsewhere." "She must have known it was happening." "She could have stopped it but chose to turn a blind eye." When the mothers of victims do discover the abuse, their responses vary. A tiny minority see it as normal and inevitable, and counsel their child to put up with it. Others, because of their partner's history of violence and abuse, feel helpless and afraid, but never give up trying to find help in the unbearable situation they find themselves in. The vast majority of mothers, however, are outraged and take whatever steps are possible to protect their child or children. Since the 1970s when sexual abuse of children was beginning to be treated as a crime, such mothers report the crime to the police and courageously begin the process of having their partner charged under the law. Needless to say, the court process is a harrowing experience for most mothers as defence lawyers are only too eager to find 'evidence' that will present the mother in a bad light.

S. Caroline Taylor, who has written extensively on the topic of child sexual abuse, highlighted the fact that there is, in society, a "propensity to punish women who accuse men of wrongdoing."[129] To illustrate that point, Taylor presented a case study in which a mother (Eileen) who had reported her husband's inappropriate sexual behaviour toward his stepdaughter, was accused by the perpetrator of having mental health issues. Following those accusations, the mother was admitted as an involuntary patient in a psychiatric facility, from which time, police and child protection agencies simply brushed her aside as someone with 'mental health issues'. Also, the small community in which Eileen lived shunned her as a woman who had falsely accused her husband, while he continued to enjoy the support of the community. Eileen lost everything – her home, children (the husband was granted custody of all five children), community, friends, job, as well as the sense of wellbeing she once enjoyed.

Ten years later, when the daughter reported long-term sexual, physical and emotional abuse by her stepfather, he was charged, convicted and imprisoned. Eileen had been right all along but, even though the stepfather finally admitted his guilt, the legal profession still found a way to lay some blame at Eileen's feet. Taylor reported:

> One of the pre-sentence reports sought by the offender's legal counsel suggested the father was in fact a victim in this case by suggesting the mother was a culpable agent and that the victim's disclosure and subsequent legal action punished the father severely. At sentencing the judge obliged by declaring the mother a 'mitigating factor' that reduced the culpability of the offender and further suggested that the victim/survivor did not suffer too greatly in his opinion.[130]

---

129 S. Caroline Taylor (2003–2004) 'Public Secrets/Private Pain: difficulties encountered by victim/survivors of sexual abuse in rural communities'. In *Women Against Violence*, p. 17.
130 *Ibid*, p. 17.

All of the studies into the effects on mothers of sexual abuse victims agree that, initially, there is shock, denial, confusion and a feeling of numbness. This initial period is followed by feelings of betrayal, hurt, fear, embarrassment, guilt and failure as a wife and mother and, for many mothers, there is the additional trauma of having to deal with the effects of their own sexual abuse by the same perpetrator. Following the pain and acknowledgement of loss and failure, there is anger – anger at the perpetrator for what he did; anger at themselves for not knowing, or not being able to stop it; and anger at their child for not telling them. In addition, there is worry about what other people will think when they find out.[131]

When the perpetrator is the child's father, stepfather, grandfather, older brother or other family member, the mother is often judged harshly by her extended family for 'bringing shame on the family' by going to the police and making the abuse public. Just when the mother most needs their support, she is forced into a situation of loneliness and isolation from those closest to her.

One particularly painful consequence of child sexual abuse is that the mother's relationship with the abused child is often damaged:

> Many children experience feelings of anger and betrayal at their mothers for not having protected them from the abuse. Girls who are sexually abused by their fathers are often angrier with their mothers than with their abusers[132]

Long-term effects suffered by many mothers of abused children include depression, anxiety, sleep problems, post-traumatic stress disorder, regret, guilt, self-recrimination and ongoing deep-seated anger.

---

131 <http://www.dvrcv.org.au/help-advice/sexual-abuse-in-childhood>
132 Carol-Ann Hooper (1992) *Mothers Surviving Child Sexual Abuse.*

So, what of Ann Hannah? What effects did she suffer as a mother of a child being sexually abused by her stepfather, Ann Hannah's husband? Looking back on the way my grandmother coped from day to day, it is not easy to identify the ways in which she was damaged by his actions. It is difficult to imagine what it must have been like for her more than a century ago – under the total domination of her husband; knowing the abuse and destruction he was wreaking on her first born daughter (and on herself); no one to turn to for help; no Women's Services; no laws in place to hold perpetrators responsible for their actions; and, consequently, feelings of utter helplessness.

If Ann Hannah had reported her husband's abuse to the authorities, she would simply have been sent home and advised to be a more loyal and obedient wife. To revisit John Stuart Mill's quote:

> In no other case (except that of a child) is the person who has been proved judicially to have suffered an injury, replaced under the physical power of the culprit who inflicted it.[133]

If she had been religious and sought help from the church, the same thing would have happened. She would have been counselled to be a good wife and to examine her own behaviour to see what *she* was doing to cause the problems her husband was having. Such a situation paints a picture of utter powerlessness.

When I ask myself what effects my grandmother may have experienced, my mind goes to the fact that she always seemed to have an essential sadness. Occasionally, friends would ask my mother if Nana was unhappy about something when she was actually just being herself. Also, when I was old enough to think about matters of self-esteem, it occurred to me that Nana seemed

---

133 Mill, p. 16.

to have a low self-esteem and a low sense of self-worth in relation to others. It may be, though it is difficult to prove, that these were effects of her experience as mother of a child being sexually abused and as a wife who was regularly raped by her husband. While it is impossible to be certain about the immediate effects on Ann Hannah, it is likely that the effects she experienced were those that have been widely documented, such as self-blame, grief, fear, powerlessness and anger.

If she interpreted his behaviour as a need for sex, she would have blamed herself for not being able to satisfy him sexually. Also, believing that a mother's role is to keep her children safe, she would have blamed herself for the dangerous situation Annie May was forced to live in.

The grief she experienced would, perhaps, have been for the loss of a normal relationship with her husband and, also, with her daughter, which his abusing behaviour rendered impossible. The grief she felt over losing her first husband would have surfaced and re-surfaced each time she pondered on how different her life could have been if James had not died at such a young age.

My mother and her sister Emily told us, years ago, that Ann Hannah was afraid of their father's violence, so fear was present too. Consequently, she would have been careful not to provoke him in an attempt to avoid any further physical and sexual violence against her and her daughter.

Her sense of powerlessness must have been palpable. With no law to protect her and her family from their abuser, no one to talk to who would believe her, no support services, no respect for women except as chattels and supporters of men, it is reasonable to assume that Ann Hannah would have experienced powerlessness on a daily basis.

It is most likely, too, that she experienced anger. In fact, I imagine that she was very angry when she first realised what was happening, but had to keep it bottled up inside knowing that there was no safe outlet for the anger she felt.

In addition to these immediate effects, there would also have been long-term effects. It's possible that she experienced regret, an emotion that is similar to, but different from, grief. Thinking of Ann Hannah's practical approach to life ("if there's a problem, you fix it"), it is not too much of a stretch to suggest that she lived with a sense of regret that she was not able to do anything to rectify the situation she found herself in throughout her marriage to Arthur Stickley.

I imagine that she experienced isolation. One thing about my grandmother that stands out in my mind is the fact that she appeared to have no friends of her own. I have no recollection of her ever attempting to meet people or develop friendships outside our home and extended family. I always imagined that it was because she was a shy, quiet, unassuming kind of person. But now, focusing my attention on the isolation Arthur Stickley forced on her – separating her from her mother and ten siblings when he insisted on emigrating to Australia and, more importantly, causing her to live for many years with the terrible secret that her husband was sexually abusing her first-born daughter (and raping her) – I am convinced that isolation became a state that she chose for herself.

She may also have felt hatred. My own view, as someone who is committed to justice, is that hatred is sometimes appropriate, in particular, hatred of those who persist in perpetrating acts of evil, violence and abuse. My sister Beverley told me that, one day, when she and our grandmother were talking in general about marriage and children, Nana said in her usual quiet, off-hand way: "'appiest day o' my life when 'e died." For Ann Hannah, who never really talked freely about personal feelings, such a statement was an expression of the hatred she still felt for Arthur

Stickley decades after his death. The day he died was, indeed, the happiest day of her life.[134]

I began this chapter by stating my belief that the exploration of this particular saying would allow me to get to the heart of who Ann Hannah was. And that is exactly what I think has happened. Throughout my younger years, I knew my grandmother as quiet and introverted, never putting herself forward, never demanding attention, seeming content to lurk in the shadows, as it were. I also saw her as totally focused on the family, with few, if any, outside interests or connections. Rather, she saw her role as assisting Mum with cooking, cleaning and child-minding. It also seemed to me that she was not very emotional, at least not expressing emotions. She rarely said an angry word (occasionally she did seem to be angry, but always kept a tight rein on it), and I can't remember ever seeing her cry.

All through my childhood and young adult years, when I lived at home, I just accepted that that was the way my grandmother was and never thought to question it. Years later, when I developed a feminist consciousness, I began to wonder why she didn't seem to have a mind of her own and why she chose rarely to exercise her own will. I decided that it was due to the fact that women of her era were not expected to have independent opinions, nor were they encouraged to take leadership roles even within the family.

However, having explored, in this chapter, all of the ramifications of living with the man she called 'wickid', I see that, while all of that was no doubt true, there was much more to it. My grandmother, Ann Hannah, was as she was because of the

---

134 From all I know about the recidivism of child sexual abusers, it is clear to me that, for my sisters, my two girl cousins and me, the day he died was the *luckiest* day of our lives. He died a few years before we were born and, with his death, went any possibility of his abusing us in the same way he had abused his stepdaughter Annie May, and his daughter Emily.

many years that her life was dominated by a selfish, self-centred bully of a husband who perpetrated physical and sexual violence against her and sexual abuse against her daughter. Like so many women of her time, she had no recourse, no help, no voice and no justice. Her response, as will be discussed in the final chapter, was to accept her lot and get on with the business of living her life in the best possible way.

CHAPTER FIVE

"That's my Albert"

At age 34, Ann Hannah gave birth to a son whom she called Albert. There is no indication that she had a preference for the sex of any of her children but after having three daughters, I imagine that the birth of a baby boy must have been cause for great excitement. Albert was born in 1915 when Britain was in the throes of World War I.

Perhaps Ann Hannah called her son Albert after the late husband and Prince Consort of the reigning monarch, Queen Victoria. History records that, on the death of Prince Albert, the grief of Queen Victoria was so deep and prolonged that it was felt by the whole nation and continued for the whole of her long reign:

> On the 14 December 1861, Albert, the Prince Consort, died. He was only 42. His unexpected death plunged Queen Victoria into grief so overwhelming that it endured for the rest of her life. Her pain was shared by the nation in an outpouring of angst that would not be seen again until the death, 136 years later, of Princess Diana.[135]

---

135 <http://www.historyinanhour.com/2011/12/14/death-of-prince-albert/>

Albert Stickley (1915–1932) was born in England and migrated to Australia with his family when he was six years old. He died in Australia at age eighteen following a battle with Bright's Disease, which is an old term for diseases of the kidney[136] now known as nephritis. I can't remember my mother or grandmother ever talking at any length about Albert, probably due to the fact that neither my siblings nor I ever asked about him. In more recent years, on the death of a child, some people choose to prepare a kind of journal recording the story of the child's life so that, even though that child's sojourn on earth was short, his/her existence is recorded and passed on to future generations. I was never aware of any written record of Albert's life and, with so little discussion about him in the years following his death, the memory of his existence faded sooner than it should have.

The only time I remember Ann Hannah ever mentioning his name in my hearing was when we were sitting together looking at old family photos. We were laughing at some of the things in the photos like hairstyles and clothes. One of us pointed at a boy in a photo and asked: "Who's that Nan?" Lowering her eyes and her voice, she said "That's my Albert." As a child, I wasn't able to understand the significance of her reaching out and gently touching the boy in the photo nor of the change in her demeanour, but the fact that I have never forgotten the words nor the emotion expressed in those words reveals that it was very significant indeed. None of us said anything. We just paused for a moment and then continued looking through the photo collection.

Many years later, after slowly piecing together the bits of information that came my way in the normal course of family

---

136 Interestingly, my mother, who was three years older than her brother Albert, died as a result of polycystic kidney disease but, thankfully, she lived until she was 69.

conversations, I realised that Ann Hannah, mother of three daughters and one son, had cared for her son as he struggled with kidney disease, and then watched him die at age eighteen. Her youngest child. Her only son. How did she cope with such a personal tragedy?

Many parents who have experienced the heartbreak of losing a child refer to it as "the pain that never goes away." Some choose to write about their experience on websites set up for that purpose and a search of the web reveals many poignant examples.

In an article 'What I Wish More People Understood About Losing A Child', published on the mindbodygreen website, Paula Stephens tells of her experience four and a half years after the death of her oldest son. She says:

> Losing a child is the loneliest, most desolate journey a person can take, and the only people who can come close to appreciating it are those who share the experience.

She asks those who have never had the experience of losing a child to:

- *Remember our children*. "We want the world to remember our child or children … (If you knew Brandon) please tell me you remember him. One of my greatest joys is talking about Brandon."
- *Accept that you can't 'fix' us*. "Please don't tell us it's time to get back to life, that it's been long enough, or that time heals all wounds. We welcome your support and love … but our sense of brokenness isn't going to go away."
- *Know that there are at least two days a year that we need time out*. "Birthdays are especially hard for us … and the anniversary date of when our child died …"
- *Remember that we struggle every day with happiness*. "It's an ongoing battle to balance the pain and guilt of outliving your child with a desire to live in a way that honors them and their time on earth."

While acknowledging that grieving parents can and do still

experience happy times, Paula Stephens goes on to say: "We will never forget our child. And in fact, our loss is always right under the surface of other emotions, even happiness."[137]

On a different website, 'A Working Grief', another mother tells her story of loss and coping:

> Two years and 9 days ago, my beautiful daughter died. Two years and 9 days ago my world fell apart, and time has changed little. There are still no days without tears, NOT A SINGLE DAY …
>
> Yes, I look 'better' as I 'appear' to be living life, but few know what thoughts run through my head or what pains I feel in every part of my body. Few know the anxiety that now envelopes my life each day and the terror that overcomes me when I fully realize that we picked out a casket for our girl, stroked her hair and kissed her cold cheek before we put her in the ground, and can't hold her in my arms. Few understand the inability to breathe each time I do something with anyone else that I know I can't do with Melinda. The feeling that I'm going to lose my mind is never far away.
>
> I have tried to push myself to face all that I have been avoiding since Melinda's accident. I've avoided her favourite places, the places we visited together, the craftroom we spent hours in together, and so much more. These days I'm trying to visit those places and not go crazy. Today I decided to listen to a piece of music Melinda loved. Music has been very difficult for me. It depicts a time of joy, when life was promising. Now it's just painful. She had chosen this as the song she would walk down the aisle to, but instead it was the last piece of music we played at her funeral …
>
> I'm trying to remember without all the disabling pain; I'm trying to remember all the love and happiness we shared with Melinda, but I'm not there yet. Two years and 9 days later, I'm still broken but the world keeps moving on.[138]

---

137 These three quotations are taken from Paula Stephens' article at <http://www.mindbodygreen.com/0-17928/what-i-wish-more-people-understood-about-losing-a-child.html>

138 <https://workinggrief.wordpress.com/>

Many parents struggling to come to terms with the death of their child find a degree of comfort in expressing their grief publicly and, in recent decades, the internet has afforded them that platform. Writing about their child, recalling happy times, expressing their deep grief, can be therapeutic and can form the background to future growth. Of course, it must all happen in its own time because acceptance and growth will only occur when the person who is grieving feels emotionally ready.

As I attempt this psychological analysis of Ann Hannah's grief and explore the opportunities she may have had to express her grief in a psychologically healthy way, I am convinced that her experience of grief at the loss of her precious Albert would have been no less harrowing and heartbreaking than those expressed above: extreme sadness, constant pain, loneliness, desolation, brokenness, guilt (at having outlived her child), anxiety, the need for private time to grieve, the need to ensure that her child's time on earth is remembered, and confusion that, even though something as catastrophic as losing her child has occurred, the world simply moved on.

Thinking now about my grandmother's experience of losing Albert, my mind goes to my own work as a practising psycho-therapist from 1980 to 2010. During that time, I did much work around grief and loss, and developed my own way of assisting clients who came to talk about their constant, unrelenting grief. Most knew that they had to 'move on' eventually, but acknowledged that they were stuck. In fact, many admitted that they did not actually want to move on because, in their minds, it would entail leaving their loved one behind. Some said that it felt like a kind of betrayal to move beyond the life they had shared with the one they had lost. Even the decision to seek the help of a therapist was frightening since they realised it was an acknowledgement that they wanted to find a way to move on regardless of how that might affect their memory of times past. For the sake of their own mental health, however, it had to be done.

As I sought to develop my ability to help in the area of grief and loss, I remember being most affected by, and impressed with, Elisabeth Kübler-Ross' book *On Death and Dying*,[139] in which she postulated five stages of grief that terminally-ill patients go through in order to reach a point of acceptance and achieve a peaceful death. The five stages are: denial and isolation, anger, bargaining, depression, and acceptance.

Many terminally-ill patients still find this a helpful way to look at their situation because it helps them come to an understanding of the emotional and psychological reactions they are experiencing. In my work with people experiencing grief over the loss of a loved one, however, I found that the stages of grief were somewhat different for them. Rather than having to confront their own impending death, they were confronting the spectre of having to live on into the future without a person who they had loved dearly.[140]

With Kübler-Ross' stages as a guide, I developed a series of stages to help my clients navigate their way through the devastating experience of loss they were confronting. I have always believed that *knowledge* has an important role to play in restoring mental and emotional equilibrium and, consequently, I wanted to arm people with knowledge of the stages a grieving person must go through in order to regain their sense of health and wellbeing. They needed to have a clear understanding of their situation, why they feel the way they do at any given time, and

---

139 Elisabeth Kübler-Ross (1969) *On Death and Dying*.

140 While my focus here is deliberately on loss through death of a loved person, I acknowledge that grief and a sense of loss covers a broad range of experiences: loss through separation and divorce; loss of a precious pet; loss of employment; loss of physical and mental ability; and so on.

what to expect to feel in the future. Such information, sensitively delivered by a therapist, can help shed light on a path that most have not travelled before. There is a grieving *process* and, while it varies according to individual need, the process toward healing after loss and the restoration of a sense of mental and emotional wellbeing is similar for everyone.

The stages of grief I often observed were:

1. *Shock, denial, relief, numbness, isolation.* The emotions people experience on hearing news of a loved one's death usually vary according to circumstance, and can include any or all of the above. When a loved one dies suddenly as in a car accident, suicide or murder, shock and denial are felt very keenly. On the other hand, for those who lose a loved one after a long illness, when death has long been anticipated, while they may experience some element of shock and denial that death has finally come, the main emotion is often relief – relief that their loved one is no longer suffering and relief that they themselves no longer have to stand by helplessly and observe the decline and suffering of the person they love.

   Numbness is not experienced by every grieving person but many do use the word to describe their inability to feel anything in the early days and weeks of grieving. The need to attend to practical issues (making funeral arrangements, notifying friends and family members, etc.) is important because such practical tasks keep a grieving person occupied and focused immediately after the death. It is in the period after the funeral, when friends and relatives have gone back to their normal lives, that one can experience a kind of numbness. If the grieving is normal and healthy, the period of numbness will pass when the time is right but, if pressure to move on is applied by those who desperately want their friend to focus on all the positive feelings they could and 'should' be having, the danger is that the numbness could become entrenched, and may even stand in the way of the person moving on.

Isolation refers to the decision many grieving people make to isolate themselves from others for a time. This is a healthy choice that, again, should be allowed to continue for as long as it takes. As with numbness, however, if the need for social isolation becomes entrenched and takes on the appearance of agoraphobia or other anxiety-related conditions, she or he may need to seek psychological intervention.

2. *Deep sadness, depression.* Whatever form the initial response to a loved one's death takes, there is always sadness. Sometimes the sadness is deep and unrelenting, sometimes it feels more manageable but initially, it is a constant companion. It is important to remember that sadness is a normal emotion that everyone can expect to feel at different times throughout life. In this neoliberal era, when market forces often seem to take precedence over ethical business practices, the advertising of products promising to keep everyone young, fit, healthy and happy, is aimed at convincing people that eternal happiness is possible when, of course, it is not. A healthy person is one who experiences a whole range of emotions and whose emotions are kept in balance. It is the *balance* of emotions that makes life meaningful, interesting and satisfying.

A grieving person should expect to feel sad and, in fact, welcome it as a normal and appropriate emotion. Crying is a natural and positive way to express sadness. Some people worry that they haven't been able to cry or 'haven't cried enough'. Emotions are natural and should never be forced. They will come. Television dramas often portray examples of people who have not been able to cry 'enough' over the death of their child/partner/parent and who suddenly and surprisingly cry uncontrollably a few months or years later over the death, for example, of a neighbour's dog. It is not clear why it occasionally happens like that but, when it does, it is important that the person understands and acknowledges the transference of grief that has taken place, because it will allow the resolution of their real grief to occur sooner.

After what seems to many to be a 'respectable' period of grieving, sadness that has not been expressed can, and often does, turn into depression. It is no exaggeration to say that most grief counselling I have been involved in started with a person presenting with depression. The process leading to a person seeking counselling usually happens like this: The death of a loved one (whether sudden or anticipated) causes deep sadness and grief. After a period of grieving, the grief-stricken person is urged by others or, perhaps, by themselves to 'move on'. Not wanting to cause discomfort or distress to others, or believing it is what they ought to do, the person who is grieving will make the effort to move on with their lives, whether or not they feel ready. They suppress their feelings in an effort to give the appearance that they are over their grief and getting on with life. When that occurs, the scene is set for depression to begin, because depression is often the way suppressed feelings find expression. It must be emphasised here that anti-depressant medication is not the entire answer when unresolved grief is at the root of a person's depression. Therapy, on the other hand, can be most helpful. Many working in the field of mental health recommend a combination of medication and therapy.

In the case of grief therapy, a skilled therapist works with a depressed person to discover what it is that has been denied expression. Once the lid is taken off and the sadness and unresolved grief are allowed to flow freely, the depression lifts and healing begins.

3. *Anger.* The third stage of grief as I have observed is the expression of anger and, for many people, this is the most

difficult stage of all. The very nature of death seems to demand respect, hushed voices and an attitude of submission but, when anger is lurking below the surface in someone who is grieving, it must be expressed. So strong is the taboo against expressing anger as part of the grieving process that it is often the suppression of anger rather than of sadness that is at the root of a person's depression.

In therapy, I encourage grieving clients to explore their anger. Some are angry at a particular doctor or at the hospital system in general "for not giving the right kind of care." Some are angry at the driver of the car who "knew he shouldn't have been driving so fast." Some are angry at their husband/wife/partner for not being at the hospital when their son died. Some are angry at the person who died "for leaving me so soon." Some are angry with God.

Even as people express such feelings in therapy, they admit that they are not rational feelings and, in many cases, that is the reason people keep their anger inside and allow it to smoulder and fester and turn into depression. In these situations, the task of counselling is to help clients see that, by their very nature, emotions are not rational. Anger certainly is not rational but it must be acknowledged and released.

In order for a person's expression of anger to be most effective, the therapist needs to assess the types of expression the client feels most comfortable with and avoid situations which may seem phony or cause embarrassment. Expression through writing, drawing and poetry are options that can be explored. One counselling technique that has worked well for me with many clients has been my request that they write a letter to the person they are angry with, expressing their anger as comprehensively and convincingly as possible. They are asked to find some time during the coming week when they can be alone, to sit down and focus on the person and the reasons for their anger, and then write a very angry letter to that person. The letter is not meant to be sent to the person it is aimed at, and for that reason the client is free to let all their anger out. S/he is asked to bring the letter to the next therapy session and read it to the therapist. This technique affords the client two opportunities to express the anger – one, as the letter is being written and, two, as it is being read aloud to the therapist.

When a person suppresses anger, it is often the case that other emotions are also suppressed, so the appropriate expression of anger unblocks *all* of the emotions a grieving person has kept locked up inside following the death of their loved one.

4. *Dealing with unfinished business.* There are several reasons grieving people might have unfinished business with the person who died. When the death is sudden and unexpected, there are all the things that could have been said – an expression of love; an apology for something; gratitude for the joy s/he brought; and so on. When the death is expected after an illness, one can be left with unfinished business that is negative due to the fact that confrontations of a negative nature with someone who is dying would have seemed unkind and inappropriate.

In order to move through to a resolution of one's grief after a loved one has died, unfinished business must be attended to. Some decide to visit the grave and talk out loud to their loved one, expressing anger or love, saying sorry, asking for forgiveness, talking about anything that needs to find expression, until such time as the unfinished business can be laid to rest. Some decide to write it in a letter, a poem or a series of poems. *How* one decides to express unfinished business is of no consequence. The important thing is that it is acknowledged and expressed.

5. *Acceptance, looking to the future.* When there is no longer anything blocking the free and healthy expression of grief, the way is open for acceptance. Sadness will usually continue at some level but it is manageable and normal, and the expectation is that it will become less intense with the passing years. Once a person who is grieving has worked through the earlier stages of grief successfully and accepted that the loss has occurred, they will then have a sense that it is time to look to the future and focus on living the life they had planned to live.

In an attempt to reach some understanding of how Ann Hannah coped with the personal tragedy of losing her teenage son, I revisited the situation of her life at that time. From the testimonies of other grieving mothers, it is clear that she would have needed time alone, time to grieve, time to cry, time to remember the birth of her beautiful baby boy, time to recall memories of his childhood and teenage years, time to be angry that life was simply moving on without him and time to come, eventually, to a state of acceptance and peace and healing within herself.

The conclusion I have arrived at is that while my grandmother, Ann Hannah, would have had little time to work through her grief, she would have snatched moments of alone time where she could do just that. Her husband, Arthur Stickley, who was a demanding husband at the best of times, was in fact very ill with consumption (the old name for tuberculosis) at the time of Albert's death and he died the following year in 1933. One can imagine that Ann Hannah would have been expected to put aside her need to grieve for Albert and focus on her husband and his needs. Indeed, she would have expected it of herself. I wonder what it must have been like for her, attending to the needs of the man she had come to hate because of his long-time sexual abuse of her oldest daughter and his physical and emotional abuse of the entire family (including herself), but she would have done it because, in line with the expectations of the day, it was her duty as his wife to make sure his needs were met.

In addition to her husband's needs, Ann Hannah would have been aware of the needs of her three daughters aged in their early to mid-twenties. They had lost their brother at a time when they, themselves, were looking forward to happy and exciting futures. She would have supported them and they, in turn, would have been a comfort and support to her. As I think about this, I recall examples of my mother's care and concern for her mother through all the years that she lived as part of our family (when she expressed concern that Nana may have felt excluded at certain family gatherings; when she was upset about the way one of her sisters spoke to their mother; when Nana appeared to be sick but refused to give in to it; and so on), so I have no doubt that the support between Ann Hannah and her daughters as they all grieved for the loss of Albert would have been mutual. They would have helped each other through an intensely difficult time.[141]

While Arthur Stickley's death brought relief and a sense of freedom to Ann Hannah, it is fairly certain that, notwithstanding the support of her daughters, her grief over the death of Albert would have taken a long time to be resolved. Consistent with the quiet, no fuss, way she dealt with other events in her life, I presume that she worked through it in her own time. It is probable that she felt relief that Albert's suffering was over, but struggled with

141 On a happy note, it was during one of Albert's stays in hospital that Ann Hannah's youngest daughter, Lil (my mother), met the man she would later marry. On one visit to see her brother, Lil caught the eye of the young man in the next bed to Albert's. Dave McLellan was hospitalised following an accident at work and, as the story goes, there was an instant spark between the two. My parents married in December 1933.

a persistent sadness deep inside her. She would have experienced isolation caused by her own determination to deal with her grief in her own way. Thinking about the healing potential in anger, it would be reasonable to assume that she did feel anger but there were no stories from her daughters to suggest that she directed any anger toward them. Also, there was no indication of cruelty or sarcasm. Perhaps, after her husband's death the following year, she aimed her anger at him in her mind, remembering times when he had ignored Albert or treated him harshly. It is difficult to know if, or how, she dealt with any unfinished business she may have had with Albert, but there are strong indications that she eventually came to an acceptance of his death.

When I look at the way life proceeded for her once she became a widow, I realise that the birth of my brother Ron could have provided Ann Hannah with some hope for a positive future. Albert died in 1932, her husband Arthur died in 1933, my parents married in December 1933 and Ron was born in February 1935. Helping care for her first grandson, watching him develop and being there for him when he needed her, would, I'm sure, have contributed greatly to the healing of her grief over losing her own son.

My sisters and I always joked with Ron that he was Nana's favourite even though there really wasn't much physical evidence of favouritism, and Ron, knowing that he didn't stand much of a chance arguing with three younger sisters when they were determined to gang up on him, would just laugh it off. I realise now that it is most probable, given the fact that her loss of Albert would still have been so raw for her, that Ron was indeed very special to our grandmother.

As I continued to ponder on Ann Hannah's experience of grief, it occurred to me that her familiarity with grief would have enabled her to be especially supportive and helpful to my parents several years later when they were confronted with the possibility of losing my older sister, Joan, at eleven years of age. When Joan was diagnosed with early-onset diabetes and admitted to hospital, a dark gloom descended on our home. Mum and Dad knew nothing of the condition and, when the specialist explained that Joan would have to be injected with insulin twice a day for the rest of her life and be on a strict diet, I think a kind of grief set in as they contemplated the worst possible scenario. Bev and I, as the younger children, were not included in the conversations the adults had, but, looking back on it now, I realise that fear and dread overtook our once happy home. Mum had to be taught how to give injections so, in addition to visiting Joan in hospital every day, she would receive lessons from a nurse. (I remember her actually practising at home by drawing water into a syringe and administering the injection into an orange!). She knew that Joan would not be discharged from hospital until she had perfected the art of giving injections, so Mum worked hard at getting it right as quickly as possible.

How did the rest of us fare while our parents were totally focused on Joan and the fear of losing their oldest daughter? As I recall, apart from the different atmosphere in our home, things seemed to proceed as normal, and that would have been possible only because Ann Hannah rose to the occasion and filled all the gaps. She made our breakfast, prepared our lunches, ironed our clothes, and sent us off to school. After school, she greeted us with food and took much more responsibility than usual for preparing the evening meal. While her support of my parents would not have been expressed in words (because that was not her way), she gave them what she probably wished for herself during her time of grieving for the loss of Albert – space, quietness and lots of practical help.

It would seem now that fears of Joan's demise at age eleven were much exaggerated. Thanks to the efforts of our parents and grandmother, and to Joan's own determination to think positively about life with Type 1 diabetes, she has lived a full and productive life. There was never a time when she relaxed her diet; she began administering her own insulin injections at a young age; and married and gave birth to three healthy children. At age 71, Diabetes Australia presented her with a medal marking 60 years of living with diabetes and, next year, when she will be 81, we are anticipating she will receive the 70-year medal! We, her siblings, as well as her children and their families, are proud beyond words.

Maybe Joan's determination to conquer the negative things life threw at her came from her grandmother Ann Hannah who, with grit and determination, pulled herself through the dark years following Albert's death and went on to live a seemingly happy life until her death at age 97.

CHAPTER SIX

"Just get on with it"

In my inquiry into those sayings of Ann Hannah that had a lasting impression on me, I have saved my discussion of this one until last because it seems to shed light on how my grandmother was able to endure the pain and distress reflected in some of the previous chapters. The question that nagged at me as I analysed and discussed Ann Hannah's pride in being a 'Londoner', her forced emigration to Australia, her powerlessness in the face of her second husband's constant and long-term sexual abuse of his step-daughter and herself, and her despair over the early death of her much-loved son Albert was: How did she survive?

There are stories of women throughout history who survived by rebelling against their powerlessness and confinement, and fought to live independent lives. Conversely, there are examples of women who have surrendered to their powerlessness and been so eaten up with hatred and bitterness that they have fallen into depression and lived the whole of their lives in a state of dependence on medication and other mental health treatments. But Ann Hannah neither rebelled against the powerlessness she experienced, nor allowed herself to wallow in bitterness and hatred. The grandmother I knew never seemed to be depressed, never appeared to be on the brink of exploding with anger, never argued at any length with either of my parents. How is it that she was able to appear so contented with life? I think the answer lies in the philosophy represented by her words: "Just get on with it!"

This was always our grandmother's response whenever I or one of my siblings attempted to confide in her about certain 'injustices'. For example, to turn to her for support when our mother insisted that we clean our rooms was pointless because her response was always: "Just get on with it." Or to complain that our teachers had given us too much homework: "Just get on with it." Or that it wasn't my turn to wash the dishes when my father was insisting that I do it: "Just get on with it." Ann Hannah showed no mercy! We learnt from her that there are things in life that no amount of complaining will change, and that the only thing to do is "get on with it" the best way we could. That was her philosophy, and it seems certain that it was that attitude that enabled her to pick herself up every time and go on living regardless of the knocks. Educators and psychologists today are calling it 'resilience'.

Nelson Mandela is quoted as saying: "Do not judge me by my successes. Judge me by how many times I fell down and got back up again."[142] Echoing Mandela, Ann Hannah could say:

> Do not judge me by my seeming acquiescence to a dominant and violent husband. Do not judge me as someone who expressed little or no emotion in the face of the traumatic circumstances of my life. Judge me by how many times life knocked me down and I got back up again.

When modern-day educators and psychologists refer to this ability to keep on going in the face of adversity as resilience, they present resilience as a most desirable attribute that can and ought to be taught to children. I had never thought of my grandmother as resilient until I began this psychological analysis of different

---

142 <www.metafilter.com/114354>

aspects of her life. The general, mostly unspoken, assessment in our extended family was that "nothing seems to upset her" or "she doesn't seem to feel very deeply." But now it seems clear to me that what we were witnessing was a woman who had said to herself from quite a young age (maybe in her early twenties following the death of her first husband, James): "Just get on with it."

An interesting point about resilience is that, for all the focus today on *teaching* resilience, it does in fact come naturally for most people. Ann Hannah certainly demonstrated resilience without the need for any formal teaching or training. No matter how often life dealt her crushing blows, she would pick herself up again and get on with it.

Most of the articles I've read about resilience include helpful definitions. The American Psychological Association, for example, defines it like this:

> Resilience is the process of adapting well in the face of adversity, trauma, tragedy, threats or significant sources of stress – such as family and relationship problems, serious health problems or workplace and financial stressors. It means 'bouncing back' from difficult experiences.[143]

From the journal, *Psychology Today*:

> Resilience is that ineffable quality that allows some people to be knocked down by life and come back stronger than ever. Rather than letting failure overcome them and drain their resolve, they find a way to rise from the ashes.[144]

Other definitions I have found useful include:

> Resilience is the happy knack of being able to bungy jump through the pitfalls of life.[145]

---

143 <http://www.apa.org/helpcenter/road-resilience.aspx>
144 <https://www.psychologytoday.com/basics/resilience>
145 A. Fuller (1998) *From Surviving to Thriving: Promoting Mental Health in*

(It is the) capacity of a system to absorb disturbance, undergo change and still retain essentially the same function, structure, identity, and feedbacks.[146]

Resilience is a broad conceptual umbrella, covering many concepts related to positive patterns of adaption in the context of adversity.[147]

As I read some of the literature on resilience, I was interested to observe the focus on building resilience in children. In an article, 'Why Study Resilience?' Sam Goldstein and Robert B. Brooks explain:

The belief … is that every child capable of developing a resilient mind-set will be able to deal more effectively with stress and pressure, to cope with everyday challenges, to bounce back from disappointments, adversity, and trauma, to develop clear and realistic goals, to solve problems, to relate comfortably with others, and to treat oneself and others with respect.[148]

In Australia, the Victorian Education Department suggests a model for building resilience in children and young people that urges teachers and parents to help them develop self-awareness, self-management, social awareness and social management.[149]

These four points encapsulate most of the recommendations in other literature and on websites that focus on the value of building resilience in children and teenagers. The teaching of self-awareness is of primary importance, they say, because it encompasses the need to know who you are, be honest with

Young People. p. 75.

146 The Resilience Alliance (2011), para 9, <www.resalliance.org/resilience>

147 A.S.Masten & J. Obradovic (2006) 'Competence and resilience in development'. p. 14.

148 Sam Goldstein and Robert B. Brooks (Eds.) (2005) *Handbook of Resilience in Children,* p. 4.

149 <www.education.vic.gov.au/Documents/about/department/resilienceexeclitreview.pdf>

yourself, believe in yourself, build self-esteem, and be aware of your own needs.

Self-management is important too in that it helps in the development of self-confidence, assertiveness, self-discipline, decision-making capability and, also, emphasises the need to take care of yourself physically (adequate sleep, healthy diet and physical exercise).

The teaching of social awareness is included because it encourages children and teenagers to be aware of the needs of others, develop empathy, be aware of social and global issues, and develop the ability to analyse social and global events.

Social management, coupled with social awareness, encourages children and teenagers to make connections with other people (i.e., have friends and acquaintances), develop a sense of responsibility for others, and develop an attitude of hope for the future.

Not surprisingly, the literature purporting to help adults build resilience within themselves includes the same attributes as those outlined in suggestions for building resilience in children. The American Psychological Association brings them all together and urges adults to nurture a positive view of themselves (self-esteem), take care of themselves, look for opportunities for self-discovery (self-awareness), make connections with others (accept their help when offered and, also, respond to their need for help), take decisive actions (self-confidence, assertiveness, decision-making), accept that change is a part of living, avoid seeing crises as insurmountable problems, keep things in perspective, develop goals (have a purpose), and maintain a hopeful outlook.[150]

---

150 <http://www.apa.org/helpcenter/road-resilience.aspx>

In thinking about resilience in adults with a view to comparing other people's experience with that of Ann Hannah, my mind was drawn first to high-profile examples that continue to inspire women and men all around the world.

Nelson Mandela

The courage and resilience of Nelson Mandela (1918–2013) brought him international acclaim as a fearless activist for human rights. Born in Mvezo, Cape Province, South Africa, he became an anti-apartheid revolutionary, politician, and philanthropist, who served as President of South Africa from 1994–1999. Throughout the 1950s, Mandela worked as a lawyer supporting increasingly militant anti-apartheid organisations. Repeatedly arrested for his activism, his arrest in 1962 led to his conviction for "conspiracy to overthrow the state."[151] At his trial he said:

> I have fought against white domination, and I have fought against black domination. I have cherished the ideal of a democratic and free society in which all persons will live together in harmony and with equal opportunities. It is an ideal which I hope to live for and to achieve. But if it needs be, it is an ideal for which I am prepared to die.[152]

Sentenced to life imprisonment, he served 27 years, first on Robben Island, then Pollsmoor Prison and, later, Victor Verster Prison. Following a long international campaign and escalating civil unrest, he was released in 1990.

On his release, far from being beaten down by so many years in custody, Mandela immediately joined negotiations with South Africa's President F.W. de Klerk to abolish Apartheid and establish multiracial elections. In the 1994 election, Mandela led

---

151 <adst.org/2014/04/nelson-mandelas-road-to-the-presidency/>
152 Mandela's Rivonia Trial Speech, 1964. <https://www.nelsonmandela.org/news/entry/i-am-prepared-to-die>

the African National Congress (ANC) to victory and became the first black president of South Africa. Following more than a quarter of a century in prison, Nelson Mandela's resilience was remarkable.[153]

Lindy Chamberlain-Creighton

In Australia, New Zealand and the United States, Lindy Chamberlain's resilience is well known. Born in New Zealand in 1948, Lindy's parents moved to Australia when she was twenty months old. She married Pastor Michael Chamberlain in 1969. Life proceeded normally for Lindy and Michael until they went on a family holiday in 1980 with their two small sons and nine-week-old daughter, Azaria. Camping at a campground near Ayers Rock (now called Uluru), baby Azaria was taken from their tent by a dingo. Totally distraught at the loss of their baby, Lindy and Michael received very little sympathy from the Australian public and, in particular, from the Australian media. Arrested, tried and convicted of the murder of her daughter, Lindy was sentenced to life in prison with hard labour. Her fourth child Kahlia was born in prison in 1982 and placed in the care of her father.

In 1986, when pieces of clothing Azaria had been wearing at the time of her disappearance were found, showing clear evidence that baby Azaria had, indeed, been taken by a dingo, Lindy was released from prison immediately and the government established a Royal Commission. In 1987, the commission found her innocent of the charges. After much pressure from Lindy and her supporters, the criminal convictions against Lindy Chamberlain were finally quashed in September 1988.[154]

Following her divorce from Michael, Lindy met and married Rick Creighton in 1992 while on a speaking tour of the United

153 <adst.org/2014/04/nelson-mandelas-road-to-the-presidency>
154 <http://lindychamberlain.com/the-story/timeline-of-events/>

States. By all accounts, the marriage is a happy one and the couple now lives in Australia's Hunter Valley.

From the depths of despair – grieving over the tragic death of her baby daughter, then being convicted of her daughter's murder and spending years in prison for a crime she did not commit – Lindy Chamberlain-Creighton has risen from the ashes in spectacular fashion. Today, she conducts seminars and lectures on topics including grief and forgiveness, the responsibility of the media to report fairly, dealing with stress, describing prison life, finding faith beyond religion, etc. She is also writing a book for children and has plans to write about grief and forgiveness. She is a truly resilient woman.

Malala Yousafzai

The strength and resilience of the young Pakistani activist, Malala Yousafzai, is well known around the world. Born in 1997 in the Swat District of Pakistan's northwestern Khyber Pakhtunkhwa province, Malala has followed in the footsteps of her educational activist father Ziauddin Yousafzai. When he took her, at eleven years of age, to speak at the local press club in Peshawar in September 2008, she asked her audience to think about the Taliban's refusal to allow girls access to education with the words: "How dare the Taliban take away my basic right to education?" Her speech was covered by newspapers and television channels throughout the region and Malala soon became a target of the Taliban and their supporters.

On 9 October 2012, when Malala boarded her school bus, a gunman caught the bus, asked for her by name, pointed a pistol at her and fired three shots. One bullet hit her forehead and ended up embedded in her shoulder. For several days following the attack, she remained unconscious and in a critical condition. It was only when her condition improved that she was able to be moved to the UK for intensive rehabilitation. Following her recovery, and despite the Taliban's expressed intention to kill her and her father, Malala has continued her commitment to speaking out for human rights and, in particular, for equal access to education for girls and boys.[155]

On her sixteenth birthday, she addressed the United Nations and proclaimed that the efforts to silence her had failed. "The terrorists thought that they would change my aims and stop my ambitions," she said, "but nothing changed in my life, except this: weakness, fear and hopelessness died. Strength, power and courage was born."[156]

Then in 2014, she was awarded the Nobel Peace Prize, the youngest person ever to receive the award. In her Peace Prize lecture, Malala said:

> This award is not just for me. It is for those forgotten children who want education. It is for those frightened children who want peace. It is for those voiceless children who want change.
>
> I am here to stand up for their rights, to raise their voice … It is not time to pity them. It is time to take action so it becomes the last time, the last time, so it becomes the last time that we see a child deprived of education.[157]

The bullets and the further threats of the Taliban were not able to keep Malala Yousafzai down. With great resilience, she rose up with even more courage than she had before.

---

155 <www.biography.com/people/malala-yousafzai-21362253>

156 <http://www.independent.co.uk/news/world/asia/the-full-text-malala-yousafzai-delivers-defiant-riposte-to-taliban-militants-with-speech-to-the-un-8706606.html>

157 <http://www.nobelprize.org/nobel_prizes/peace/laureates/2014/yousafzai-lecture.html>

Rosie Batty

The resilience of Rosie Batty following the death of her eleven-year-old son Luke at the hands of his father is lauded around Australia and other parts of the world where her tragic story is known. Born in Nottinghamshire, England, Rosie settled in Australia in 1988. She met Greg Anderson in 1992 and they started a relationship soon after, but Rosie terminated the relationship after two years because of Greg's violence. Eight years later they resumed a brief sexual relationship during which time Rosie became pregnant and their son Luke was born in 2002.

Throughout the years of their separation, Greg had access rights to his son until one incident where he pulled a knife on Luke when they were alone in Greg's car. Rosie took the matter to the courts and Greg was then denied all visiting rights with his son. On appeal, a judge granted Greg permission to attend Luke's cricket and football matches on weekends but at no time was he to be alone with Luke. Rosie was unaware of that ruling.

One day, Greg attended Luke's cricket practice and, when the practice was over, Luke asked his mother if he could spend a few minutes with his Dad (whom he loved). What followed was the tragic incident that would change Rosie Batty's life forever. It all happened so quickly. Rosie looked across to the other side of the cricket field and saw Luke lying on the ground with his father standing by. Luke, the joy of her life, her vibrant, fun-loving eleven-year-old son, had been killed by his father.

How could Rosie ever recover? How could she go on living after such a personal tragedy? At first, she appeared to be measured and rational when I saw her interviewed on television, but then she seemed to find her anger and, from that point, was determined not to allow Luke's death to be in vain. She sought and received emotional support from those working in the field of domestic and family violence, during which time she developed a greater understanding of the dynamics at work in domestic violence.

She began speaking out about it and soon became a nationwide campaigner against domestic and family violence and an advocate for victims and survivors. She started a website[158] and, in 2014, established the Luke Batty Foundation[159] to assist women and children whose lives had been affected by domestic violence. She detailed the story of her tragedy in a book, *A Mother's Story*.[160]

In 2015, Rosie Batty was awarded Australian of the Year and has worked tirelessly to keep the issue of domestic violence front and centre in the minds of state and federal governments as well as in the community at large. In that same year, the Victorian government (her home state) established a Royal Commission into Family Violence.

On the home page of the neveralone website, there is a photo of Luke, followed by Rosie's own words: "My belief is a tragedy gives you an opportunity to make a difference. I've always admired people who do that." These simple, powerful words are a statement about resilience and speak volumes about Rosie's own remarkable resilience.

While Ann Hannah's experience was very different from that of Nelson Mandela, Lindy Chamberlain-Creighton, Malala Yousafzai and Rosie Batty, her resilience was nevertheless remarkable in its own way. Focusing on some of the descriptions of resilience highlighted in the definitions quoted earlier, there is no doubt that Ann Hannah 'bounced back', 'rose from the ashes', 'bungy jumped' every time life presented her with trauma, tragedy, stress or adversity. She had within herself the ability and the determination to get on with her life regardless of all the knocks. If resilience depended solely on the development of the

---

158 <www.neveralone.com.au>
159 <https://lukebattyfoundation.org.au>
160 Rosie Batty (2015) *A Mother's Story*.

kinds of attributes discussed in the literature, Ann Hannah would surely be disqualified, as a closer look at her level of self-esteem, self-awareness, self-confidence, social involvement and goal-setting will reveal. While there is no doubt that the development of such attributes will bolster a person's ability to be resilient in the face of adverse events, their absence is no indication that that person will automatically be destroyed by adversity. In fact, it is often the case that dealing with hardship at a younger age strengthens a person and gives them the emotional tools to deal with even greater hardship later on.

It is important to remind ourselves again that, while high profile examples of resilience are inspirational and catch people's attention, and while the development of attributes designed to boost resilience is to be desired, "resilience is ordinary, not extraordinary."[161] It is not a rare attribute found only in very strong and courageous people. It is common among people of all races and cultures. After a negative, crushing experience, most people find a way to pick themselves up and move on – changed, but not defeated. I have noticed over the years that one area that presents many people with great difficulty in terms of resilience is that of relationship breakdown. When men leave relationships, some women experience years of depression, some decide to make life as difficult as possible for their ex-partners and some constantly stalk ex-partners by phoning, texting, emailing, parking outside their workplace or place of residence and so on. When women leave relationships, some men resort to stalking, some make constant threats and some engage in actual violence toward their ex-partner which, in far too many cases, results in her death. Research shows that leaving a relationship can be a very dangerous time for a woman and her children with the numbers

---

161 American Psychological Association, "What is Resilience?"
   <http://www.apa.org/helpcenter/road-resilience.aspx>

of women murdered by their ex-partners and children murdered by their fathers increasing in recent years.[162]

Some women and men remark that it would have been easier to live with the news that their partner had died than to live with the reality that s/he had ended the relationship and moved on. Such rejection is difficult for some to bounce back from but, since it is impossible to force a person to rekindle the love they once felt, resilience is required.

To my knowledge, Ann Hannah never had to face the trauma of that kind of rejection but, while it is not helpful to compare traumas and pass judgment on levels of severity, it does seem that rejection would have been much easier for her to bear than the daily reminders of the powerlessness she experienced in her relationship with her husband, Arthur Stickley.

To test my belief that Ann Hannah's resilience came from an innate toughness strengthened by adversity, rather than from the conscious development of the kinds of attributes outlined in today's literature (self-esteem, self-awareness, self-confidence, awareness of social issues, setting goals and an attitude of hope for the future), I decided to examine each of the attributes in turn to see if and how they applied to her.

When I considered the attribute of self-esteem, for example, I couldn't help thinking that the circumstances of her childhood and place in society would surely have worked against the development of a strong sense of self. She was the eighth of eleven children born to William and Emma Payne in 1881. As the eighth child, she occupied no special place: not the oldest child, nor the oldest daughter, not the youngest child, nor the youngest

162 <http://theconversation.com/hitting-home-why-separation-is-often-the-most-dangerous-time-for-a-victim-of-domestic-violence-50650>
<http://www.aph.gov.au/About_Parliament/Parliamentary_Departments/Parliamentary_Library/pubs/rp/rp1415/Quick_Guides/DVinAust>

daughter. There is nothing to suggest that she would have received special attention. She was simply one child in a large family who, it would be safe to conclude from the employment path chosen for her, did not display any higher than average academic ability. She began working in a laundry at an early age and continued in that area throughout her working life in the United Kingdom and in Australia.

Ann Hannah's experience of school, too, would not have been conducive to the development of a strong self-esteem. From comments our grandmother made on those occasions when our family discussed schooling, she seems to have had only three or four years of formal education. As a child who spoke with a cockney accent, she would no doubt have received constant messages that she was a child of the 'lower class' and, as such, may have been reminded from time to time (by parents as well as teachers) of the need to know her 'place'.

As an adult, she would no doubt have taken for granted the prevailing view of the times that women were inferior to men. Indeed, she is not likely to have had knowledge of, or interest in, the women's uprising that was occurring in the final decades of the nineteenth century among the more privileged classes, demanding votes for women. She would simply have accepted that men were in authority, and the need for women to fight for the right to vote would never have entered her head. When the vote was finally granted to all women in the United Kingdom in 1928, Ann Hannah was already living and working in Australia. That voting in Australia is compulsory for all adult citizens was probably perplexing to her and she, no doubt, would have depended on her husband to tell her how to vote. Years after her husband's death, I have childhood memories of my grandmother asking my father on voting day who she should vote for. Dad would say things like: "You can vote however you like, so long as your vote supports the working man." He knew, as we did, that his mother-in-law would get the message!

In addition to Ann Hannah's place as eighth child out of eleven, a poor education, and her acceptance of men's authority over women, there are other circumstances that conspired against her having a healthy self-esteem. One is the fact that, as an adult, she was taken away from her aging mother, siblings, nieces, nephews and, probably, long-term friends and brought to Australia where the only people she knew, to begin with, were her husband and four children; taken from a country and culture that she was familiar with to a strange, foreign place where she knew she would have to spend the rest of her life. Personality studies reveal that a healthy self-esteem is sustained by a feeling of contentment that comes from being surrounded by supportive people and a familiarity with one's own culture. Erik Erikson wrote of the need for a sense of "sameness and continuity."[163] While familiar people and culture are not the only ingredients necessary, they do form the basis of a positive self-esteem.

The other circumstance of Ann Hannah's life that points toward the probability that her self-esteem was not strong is the fact that 'self-esteem' and 'esteem by others' almost always go hand in hand, and it is difficult to see where positive messages about herself would have come from. Her husband, Arthur Stickley, seems to have been so focused on himself that, even when he was not abusing one or more of his children or suffering the effects of alcohol, it is more than likely that he would never have bothered giving Ann Hannah positive feedback about her appearance or her work in the home or, in fact, focusing any attention at all on her needs. Women, today, who live with emotionally, physically or sexually abusive partners often find solace in, and positive feedback from, their mother or sisters or women friends. So long

163 Erikson, pp. 94–95.

as a person receives positive messages of esteem from someone or from a social or sporting group that they belong to, then a good self-esteem is possible. It is only when there is nothing positive flowing to a person that that person's opinion of themselves can take a battering. How many times do counsellors and psycho-therapists hear their women clients say something like: "I used to be such a strong, ambitious, happy person, but now I can't do anything." Constant put-downs, particularly from significant others, can cause self-esteem to drain away. For self-esteem to remain strong, a person needs to experience esteem by others.

It is possible that Ann Hannah had friends as her children were growing up and that their positive regard for her was enough to counteract the negatives coming at her from her husband but, as one of her eight grandchildren, I have no memory of meeting anyone who was primarily my grandmother's friend. Family members and friends of her children's in-laws seemed to like her very much and were always friendly toward her but they were not, first and foremost, her own friends. Nevertheless, everyone did seem to like her: her children, grandchildren, sons-in-law and their families, as well as neighbours. Maybe that was enough to sustain a degree of self-esteem. She was quietly-spoken, self-effacing, had an endearing sense of humour and seemed reasonably contented with life in all the years that I knew her.

Another attribute mentioned in the literature is self-awareness. When I think of self-awareness, I am always drawn to the quote attributed to Socrates: "The unexamined life is not worth living." Of course, Socrates' words were aimed at the citizens of his day, in particular Greek men, but they speak to me of the importance of self-awareness and self-knowledge in every generation. They warn me against just existing from one day to the next with no thought for the 'hows' and 'whys' of my existence, and no conscious analysis of 'who' I really am. In order to develop greater self-awareness and self-knowledge, there are simple questions people

135

can ask of themselves: What kind of person am I? How well do I communicate with others? What effect do my words have on others? How did I come to be the person that I am? What would I like to achieve in my lifetime? How can I leave the world a better place because of my having lived here?

It would not be true to say that Ann Hannah spent much time analysing who she was or how she was handling the circumstances of her life. In fact, indications are that she would have thought such an exercise a waste of time. She seemed to live in the moment and deal with things as they happened. The whole notion of having to work at developing self-knowledge and self-awareness would have been foreign to her. Life happened, and she got on with it.

It is also suggested that resilience requires self-confidence. No one who knew Ann Hannah would say that she had a broad-based self-confidence, but there would be agreement that she had confidence in what she knew. From my own perspective, she knew how to be a grandmother in practical terms. She never effused with love and affection but we knew, from the practical things she did, that she was a constant in our lives and could always be depended on to care for us. She knew how to be 'the extra person' in a nuclear family, never interfering with decisions my parents made and stepping back from any potential arguments about family or household matters. She fulfilled her role in the life of a busy family and had confidence in her ability to perform any household chore that presented itself.

Her confidence did not extend to analysing or discussing social and political issues. She seemed content to let the outside world manage itself while she focused on being the best she could be in her own domain or, more correctly, in the domain life had handed her.

Awareness of social issues is another attribute seen to have the ability to enhance resilience but, as mentioned, Ann Hannah exhibited a decided lack of interest in social and political issues. Maybe she believed she was not worthy of having an opinion about situations outside the narrow orbit of her own day-to-day life, or that the day-to-day struggle was all that she could handle, or maybe she had never been able to get out of the mindset of her early life – that larger issues were best left to men and, in particular, to men of a higher class than she was born into.

It must be said here that Ann Hannah's lack of interest in, and awareness of, social and political issues is not uncommon even today when globalisation has brought such issues to everyone's attention through old and new media. Still today, the majority of people around the world seem to be content to focus on their own and their family's struggles and achievements. In poverty-stricken families the focus is, of necessity, on daily survival in terms of food and shelter. In families where basic survival is not a problem, the focus is often on an individual's own education or employment or entertainment or accumulation of assets, or on establishing and maintaining personal relationships.

As the literature on resilience implies, the development of an awareness of and interest in social and political issues enables a person to see their own life in a broader context, which often leads people to the conclusion that they have as much right as anyone else to comment on, or protest against, something and, in that way, to have an impact on community, national and international affairs. As useful as this may be for the building of resilience, it held little interest for Ann Hannah.

Another attribute given prominence in my reading about resilience is the ability to develop goals but, as someone who seemed to live her life one day at a time, future goal-setting would not have been something that occupied my grandmother's mind. Over all the years that I knew her, she seemed content to let life happen and respond to whatever presented itself on a day-to-day basis. In her youth, while Ann Hannah would not have consciously 'set' goals, she would have just known that she would marry and have children, because that is what women in her family and culture did. Her goals, if she did think about them consciously, probably involved being a supportive and caring wife to a husband who loved her and a good mother to her children. When she married her first husband, James, and gave birth to Annie May, she probably thought she was on the way to fulfilling her goals but, when tragedy struck and James became ill and died, she and her simple goals were thrown into turmoil.

Her second marriage seems to have been a marriage of necessity. Being alone in the world with a child to support and no financial assistance from the government would have caused any woman in her situation to see re-marriage as the only option available. I recall a comment my mother made when I was a young adult to the effect that Nana was actually interested in and attracted to Arthur's brother and that, when she realised that the brother's interest lay elsewhere, she fell into a relationship with Arthur. Given those circumstances, it does point to the fact that Ann Hannah's marriage to Arthur was one of convenience as well as of necessity. However, I imagine that her goals of being a good wife and mother continued with her second marriage.

After Arthur's death and her move to live with my parents, her goals would have been as they had always been, that of getting on with life and making the best of whatever each day brought.

Finally, the literature points out that resilience is enhanced also by an attitude of hope for the future. Thinking about this in relation to my grandmother saddens me because it reminds me of a situation that I found heart-wrenching at the time. When she was in her twilight years, late 80s and into her 90s, she developed a habit that expressed a kind of hopelessness. Whenever the word THAMES appeared on our television screen, as it did following every program produced by the British Television Production Company called 'Thames', she would say in sad, almost mournful, tones: "Oh, send me back to good old Blighty." To be able to return to her beloved London would have been a dream of hers from the moment she set foot on Australian soil at age 40. It would have been a dream, a fantasy, but not a hope, because she would have known that such a trip would never have been possible given the family's financial situation and her husband's lack of ambition to improve their finances.

There is evidence, however, that while Ann Hannah was not in a position to hope for anything more than her circumstances allowed, she was not entirely without hope. She did seem to have hope in relation to the everyday condition of her life. One example is the fact that, following the death of her husband, when her daughters were suggesting that she live with each daughter in three-monthly cycles (see Introduction), she stated very clearly her desire to live with her youngest daughter and her husband permanently. As Ann Hannah looked forward to the future with the hope of a happy and stable life, she knew that her greatest chance of happiness and stability would be with my parents, who both possessed a calmness of spirit that enabled the development of a peaceful environment.

In focusing on resilience and acknowledging the differences between Ann Hannah's resilience and those important attributes set out by those who research and teach it, I had to ask myself the obvious question: If she didn't fit the mould outlined in the psychological texts, where did Ann Hannah's resilience come from? Was it sheer determination not to be diminished by the sizeable knocks that came her way? Or just a blind acceptance of whatever life threw at her? I'm inclined to think it was both – a blind acceptance coupled with a sheer determination to "just get on with it" and be the best that she could be in all the circumstances of her life. In all probability, the toughness that enabled such resilience sprang originally from all the hardships she would have encountered at a young age, growing up in a relatively poor family in central London. From there, each of life's knocks that came her way, would only have made her stronger.

While I applaud today's focus on teaching resilience to children and teenagers, so much so that I have included it in some detail earlier, it is important to reiterate that the development of resilience is not always dependent on such teaching. It is 'ordinary, not extraordinary', and is evident in the way most people conduct their lives. Wherever it came from in my grandmother, the resilience of this remarkable woman – Ann Hannah – is to be celebrated.

Ann Hannah's Legacy

Delving into the life and imagining the emotional responses of my quiet, unobtrusive but remarkable grandmother has been an immensely satisfying and illuminating experience for me. As I conclude, I find myself asking two questions: What has the writing of this book done for me? And, in a different vein: What is Ann Hannah's legacy?

In answer to the first, very personal, question I admit that this enterprise has had a considerable impact on me. The first thing I notice is that it has made me appreciate more than ever before the harmonious, affirming atmosphere in which I grew up and, for that, I give credit to every member of my family of origin – Mum, Dad, brother, two sisters and, of course, our grandmother.

Second, it has opened my eyes to the important contribution my grandmother, Ann Hannah, made to our family life.

Next, and painfully, it has made me face up to the awful truth that my own grandfather was a perpetrator of physical and sexual violence against his wife, and a perpetrator of sexual abuse against two of his children. Forcing myself to think about that has confirmed my belief that perpetrators must be held accountable. The situation that prevailed in my grandparents' day, where a man could do as he liked in the privacy of his own home, did men no favours. Similarly, the belief held by many today that violent men need understanding and support rather than being held accountable for their behaviour is surely not the answer. Who knows, my grandfather might have changed if he had been held to account for his violence, if there had been laws in place to hold him criminally responsible. And I can only imagine how different life could have been for my grandmother and her children.

Another thing that the writing of this book has done for me is strengthen my resolve to continue working for justice for women at every level. It is my firm belief that society as a whole would benefit enormously if women's rights to equality and justice were upheld.

One other important effect of writing this book is that it has forced me to interrogate myself on why I always saw my grandmother as ordinary and unremarkable. On this point, I remind myself that feminists in every generation have to *rediscover* the truth that women's lives are anything but unremarkable. It is a truth discovered, then deliberately hidden by patriarchy, then discovered again by the next generation of feminists. According to feminist historians, women's aspirations, ideas, knowledge and achievements have been largely ignored in every generation in favour of the words and deeds of men and, when history ignores women, they are rendered virtually invisible.

With the aim of keeping men in a superior position, mainstream society has much invested in regurgitating the myth that most women live ordinary, unremarkable lives. The predominant thought is that women, in particular those who are mothers and grandmothers, while fulfilling the role 'nature' meant for them are, nevertheless, ordinary. Their role, as assigned to them in male-dominated societies, is to focus on the family, help with the maintenance of relationships and keep the family together. Most mothers and grandmothers are seen as fixtures at the centre of the family and, therefore, any needs or aspirations that they may have, are easily ignored. That is certainly how I viewed my own mother and grandmother until my exposure to feminism opened my eyes in the 1970s with simple slogans like: "Women are people too."

The other question exercising my mind as I conclude this book is: What is Ann Hannah's legacy? What contribution did she leave behind that could possibly enrich the world – not just the people who knew her, but every generation into the future? Initially, when I considered telling my grandmother's story, I wondered how I could do it in a way that would tempt others to read it. After all, I reasoned to myself, she was not a politician, a writer, a musician or a painter; not a pioneer in the field of medicine or science; not an adventurer who had exciting stories to tell; nor was she one of the early feminist activists who fought so valiantly for the rights of women. She was my 'unremarkable' grandmother, content to live a simple, modest life to the best of her ability.

As I thought about it, it occurred to me that my grandmother's experience of life reflected that of many women in every generation. It was not just her own experience but was typical of so many women throughout history and, especially, of the women of her time and situation in life. For that reason, I concluded, her story had to be told.

When thinking about legacy, the usual thing to say of 'unremarkable' women like Ann Hannah is that she brought four children into the world, three of whom lived into adulthood and bore children of their own, and so on into future generations. But I can see now that Ann Hannah's legacy is much more than that. Indeed, I think it is true to say that the legacy of most women is more than that but, because patriarchy still downplays the personal, community and global influence of women, a degree of digging is required so that their legacy can be revealed.

In this particular case, choosing the genre of psychological biography and basing my inquiry around some of my grandmother's particular sayings enabled me to bring her to life in ways that she thought not appropriate to reveal to her grandchildren during her lifetime. Her philosophy of "just get on with it" meant that she spent very little of her time talking about the past so, to discover her more fully so long after her death presented me with a challenge, but I can now say that it has been well worth the effort. I have discovered that she gave to the world a lesson in personal strength and integrity, that she left behind many examples of how to endure hardship and emerge victorious. In spite of a limited education, relative poverty in her childhood, violence perpetrated against her and her children by her husband and the loss of her beloved son, she demonstrated a resilience beyond imagination. Dogged determination, endurance, patience and a commitment to life are all part of her legacy.

Years ago, when I began focusing seriously on feminism, I remember thinking how wonderful it would be to be able to boast that my grandmother had been a suffragette which, of course, she was not. How proud I would have been! Today, however, as I present this psychological biography of my grandmother, Ann Hannah, I could not be more proud, and am deeply grateful for the example of courage and resilience she set for me.

References

Abu-Lughod, Lila (2012) 'Pushing at the Door: My Father's Political Education, and Mine', pp. 41-60 in Penny Johnson and Raja Shehadeh (Eds.) *Seeking Palestine*. North Melbourne: Spinifex Press.

American Academy of Child and Adolescent Psychiatry (2014) 'Child Sexual Abuse'. Facts for Families No. 9, <https://www.aacap.org/AACAP/Families_and_Youth/Facts_for_Families/FFF-Guide/Child-Sexual-Abuse-009.aspx>

American Psychological Association (2017) <http://www.apa.org/helpcenter/road-resilience.aspx>

Armstrong, Louise (1994) *Rocking the Cradle of Sexual Politics*. Reading, Mass.: Addison-Wesley.

Atkinson, Judy (2002) *Trauma Trails, Recreating Song Lines: The Transgenerational Effects of Trauma in Indigenous Australia*. North Melbourne: Spinifex Press.

Australian Institute of Health and Welfare (15 December 2016) 'More receiving homelessness support due to family violence', http://aihw.gov.au/media-release-detail/?id=60129557836

Australian Parliamentary Library (2015) <http://www.aph.gov.au/About_Parliament/Parliamentary_Departments/Parliamentary_Library/pubs/rp/rp1415/Quick_Guides/DVinAust>

Barlee, E (1963) *A Visit to Lancashire in December 1862*. London: Routledge and Kegan Paul.

Batty, Rosie (2015) *A Mother's Story*. Melbourne: HarperCollins.

Batty, Rosie (2016) <www.neveralone.com.au>

Batty, Rosie (2015) <https://lukebattyfoundation.org.au>

Bartley, Paula (2002) *Emmeline Pankhurst*. London: Routledge.

Bernheimer, Charles and Claire Kahane. (Eds.) (1985) *In Dora's Case: Freud-Hysteria-Feminism*. London: Virago.

Booth, Charles (1902) *Life and Labour of the People in London*. Volume I. London: Macmillan.

Bryant and May (1888) http://www.spartacus.schoolnet.co.uk/TUmatchgirls. htm

Chamberlain-Creighton, Lindy (2010) < http://lindychamberlain.com/the-story/timeline-of-events/>

Clark, H. & Quadara, A (2010) *Insights into sexual assault perpetration: Giving voice to victim/survivors' knowledge.* (Research Report No. 18). Melbourne: Australian Institute of Family Studies.

Cooper, Selina (1888) <http://www.socialistparty.org.uk/socialistwomen/sw9. htm>

d'Alpuget, Blanche (1982) *Robert J. Hawke: a Biography*. Melbourne: Schwartz in conjunction with Lansdowne Press.

d'Alpuget, Blanche (2011) *Hawke, the Prime Minister.* Melbourne: Melbourne University Press.

Daily Mail (26 June 2012) <www.dailymail.co.uk/…/Bow-Bells-mark-area-true-Londoners-drowned-capitals- noise>

Domestic Violence Resource Centre Victoria. <http://www.dvrcv.org.au/help-advice/sexual-abuse-in-childhood>

Education Victoria. https://www.google.com.au/search?client=safari&rls= en&q=%3Cwww.education.vic.gov.au/Documents/about/department/ resilienceexeclitreview.pdf%3E%3E+Need&ie=UTF-8&oe=UTF-8&gfe_ rd=cr&ei=WD1HWZGaKbLM8geeuqGADw

Easteal, Patricia (1998) 'Rape in Marriage: Has the Licence Lapsed? In P. Easteal (Ed.). *Balancing the Scales: Rape, Law Reform and Australian Culture*, pp. 107–123.

Erikson, Erik H (1980) *Identity and the Life Cycle.* New York: W. W. Norton.

Finkelhor, David and Angela Browne (1985) 'The Traumatic Impact of Child Sexual Abuse: A Conceptualization'. pp. 530–541 in *American Journal of Orthopsychiatry,* Vol. 55, Issue 4, October.

Fleming, JL (1997) 'Prevalence of childhood sexual abuse in a community sample of Australian women'. *The Medical Journal of Australia,* vol 166, issue 2, pp. 65–68, <http://europepmc.org/abstract/med/9033559>

Foreign Correspondent (26 August 2016) <www.abc.net.au/foreign/content>

Fuller, A (1998) *From surviving to thriving: Promoting mental health in young people.* Camberwell: The Australian Council for Educational Research.

Gartner, John D (2008) *In Search of Bill Clinton: A Psychological Biography.* New York: St. Martin's Press.

Ghafari, Roya and Blanca Lopez (2009) *Our Unspoken Stories: The Stories of Butterflies.* The Sexual Assault Support Centre of Ottawa SASC.

Gillespie, Mark (2008) 'Mapoon: the burning of a community', <http://www.
solidarity.net.au/7/mapoon-the-burning-of-a-community/>

Goldstein, Sam and Robert B. Brooks, (Eds.) (2005) *Handbook of resilience in
children*. New York: Kluwer Academic/Plenum Publishers.

Gordon, Neve (2008) *Israeli's Occupation*. Berkeley: University of California
Press.

Gordon, Neve (2008) 'From Colonization to Separation: exploring the structure
of Israel's occupation'. *Third World Quarterly*, Vol. 29, Issue 1, pp. 25–44.
<http://www.tandfonline.com/doi/abs/10.1080/01436590701726442>

Greer, Germaine (1989) *Daddy, We Hardly Knew You*. London: Hamish
Hamilton.

Hamilton, Cicely (1909/1981) *Marriage as a Trade*. London: The Women's
Press,

Herman, Judith (1981/2000) *Father-Daughter Incest*. Cambridge, Mass.:
Harvard University Press.

Hickson, W (1840) *Handloom Weavers Report*. Report from the Commissioners
onthe State of Handloom Weavers, London.

History in an Hour (2011) <http://www.historyinanhour.com/2011/12/14/
death-of-prince-albert/>

Hooper, Carol-Ann (1992) *Mothers Surviving Child Sexual Abuse*. London:
Routledge.

Hossain, Begum Rokeya (1880-1932). <http://nationalwomansparty.org/
womenwecelebrate/begum-rokeya-sakhawat-hossain/>

Human Rights and Equal Opportunity Commission (1997) *Bringing Them
Home: Report of the National Inquiry into the Separation of Aboriginal
and Torres Strait Islander Children from Their Families*. Canberra: The
Commonwealth of Australia.

Jordan Institute for Families (June 2000) 'The Effects of Sexual Abuse'. Vol. 5,
No. 2, <http://www.practicenotes.org/vol5_no2/effects_of_sexual_abuse.
htm>

Jordan, J (2008) *Serial Survivors: Women's Narratives of Surviving Rape*.
Annandale, NSW: The Federation Press.

Kaplan, Gisela (1992) *Contemporary Western European Feminism*. Sydney: Allen
& Unwin.

Kaplan, Gisela (1996) *The Meagre Harvest: The Australian Women's Movement
1950s–1990s*. Sydney: Allen & Unwin.

Kübler-Ross, Elisabeth (1969) *On Death and Dying*. New York: Macmillan.

Kumari, Ranjana (2016) 'A Brief History of Indian Feminism (1850–1995)',
<https://www.globalcitizen.in/en/content/ranjana-kumari-a-brief-history-
of-indian-feminism/>

Lakhani, Nina (12 April 2012) 'Scale of abuse against women revealed'. London: *The Independent.*

London County Council (1909) Report by The Conference on the Teaching of English in London Elementary Schools, https://ifind.swan.ac.uk/discover/Record/579503

London Society for Women's Suffrage (1867) <www.learningcurve.gov.uk>

Lubin, Albert J (1972/1996) *Stranger on the Earth: A Psychological Biography of Vincent van Gogh.* New York: Da Capo Press; New York: Holt & Co..

Mandela, Nelson (1964) 'I am prepared to die'. *Nelson Mandela Centre of Memory.* Nelson Mandela Foundation. <https://www.nelsonmandela.org/news/entry/i-am-prepared-to-die>

Mandela, Nelson. (2014) <adst.org/2014/04/nelson-mandelas-road-to-the-presidency/>

Mandela, Nelson (2012) <www.metafilter.com/114354>

Masson, Jeffrey (1990) *Against Therapy.* London: Fontana/Collins. First published 1989. London: William Collins Sons.

Masten, AS & J Obradovic. (2006) 'Competence and resilience in development'. *Annals New York Academy of Sciences,* Vol. 1094, pp. 13–27.

McLellan, Betty (1995) *Beyond Psychoppression: A Feminist Alternative Therapy.* North Melbourne: Spinifex Press.

Miles, Rosalind (2001) *Who Cooked the Last Supper: The Women's History of the World.* New York: Three Rivers Press.

Mill, John Stuart (1869/1970) *The Subjection of Women.* Cambridge, Mass.: MIT Press. Originally published in London: Longmans, Green, Reader, and Dyer.

Mitchell, Hannah (1902) <http://www.socialistparty.org.uk/socialistwomen/sw9.htm>

Modjeska, Drusilla (1990) *Poppy.* Ringwood, Vic: McPhee Gribble.

Nightingale, Florence (1928/1979) 'Cassandra'. In Ray Strachey (Ed.). *The Cause.* London: Virago, pp. 395–418

O'Shane, Pat (1995) 'The Psychological Impact of White Colonialism on Aboriginal People'. *Australasian Psychiatry,* Vol. 3, No. 3. pp. 149–53.

Pankhurst, Sylvia (1904) http://www.marxist.com/sylvia-pankhurst.htm

Pence, Ellen (1980) <http://www.theduluthmodel.org/pdf/PowerandControl.pdf>

Pence, Ellen and Michael Paymar (1993). *Education Groups for Men who Batter: The Duluth Model.* New York: Springer Publishing.

Pieters-Hawke, Sue (2011) *Hazel: My Mother's Story.* Sydney: Pan Macmillan Australia.

Pittaway, Eileen and Linda Bartolomei (2001) 'Refugees, Race and Gender: The Multiple Discrimination against Refugee Women'. *Refuge: Canada's Periodical on Refugees.* Vol. 19, No. 6, pp. 21–32.

Psychology Today (2017) <https://www.psychologytoday.com/basics/resilience>

Raphael, B, Swan P, and Martinek, N (1998) 'Intergenerational Aspects of Trauma for Australian Aboriginal People'. In Yael Danieli, (Ed.) *International Handbook of Multigenerational Legacies of Trauma.* New York: Plenum Press, pp. 327–39.

Rush, Florence (1980) *The Best Kept Secret: Sexual Abuse of Children.* Englewood Cliffs, New Jersey: Prentice-Hall.

Said, Edward (2001) *Reflections on Exile and other Literary and Cultural Essays.* London: Granta Books.

Shepard, Melanie F. and Ellen L. Pence (1999) *Coordinating Community Responses to Domestic Violence: Lessons from Duluth and Beyond.* Thousand Oaks, California: Sage.

Smyth, Ethel (1911) <http://www.sandscapepublications.com/intouch/marchwords.html> <http://www.youtube.com/watch?v=LCtGkCg7trY

Socialist Party (2008) <http://www.socialistparty.org.uk/socialistwomen/sw9.htm>

Spender, Dale (1982) *Women of Ideas (and what men have done to them): From Aphra Behn to Adrienne Rich.* London and Boston: Routledge & Kegan Paul.

Stopes, Charlotte Carmichael (1894) *British Freewomen: Their Historic Privilege.* London: Social Sciences Series, Swann Sonnenschein.

Strachey, James (Tr. and Ed., 24 Vols.) (1953–1974) *Standard Edition of the Complete Psychological Works of Sigmund Freud.* Vol. 1. London: Hogarth.

Stephens, Paula (2015) <http://www.mindbodygreen.com/0-17928/what-i-wish-more-people-understood-about-losing-a-child.html>

Swanson, Donna (1976) 'Minnie Remembers'. In Grana, Janice (Ed.) *Images: Women in Transition.* Nashville Tennessee: The Upper Room.

Taylor, Debbie (5 August 1984) 'Kiss Daddy Goodnight'. In *New Internationalist*, 138, <http://newint.org/features/1984/08/05/kiss/>

Taylor, S Caroline (2003–2004) 'Public Secrets/Private Pain: difficulties encountered by victim/survivors of sexual abuse in rural communities'. In *Women Against Violence.* Issue 15, pp. 12–21.

Textile Workers (1900) <http://www.bbc.co.uk/radio4/womanshour/timeline/1900.shtml>

The Conversation (26 November 2015) <http://theconversation.com/hitting-home-why-separation-is-often-the-most-dangerous-time-for-a-victim-of-domestic-violence-50650>

The Independent (12 July 2013) <http://www.independent.co.uk/news/world/asia/the-full-text-malala-yousafzai-delivers-defiant-riposte-to-taliban-militants-with-speech-to-the-un-8706606.html>

The Resilience Alliance (2011) *About RA*, Para. 9, <www.resalliance.org/resilience>

Thornbury, Walter (1873) 'Shoreditch'. In *Old and New London: Volume 2*. London: Cassell Petter & Galpin, pp. 194–195.

United Nations Relief and Work Agency for Palestine Refugees <http://www.unrwa.org/etemplate.php?id=86>

Wallace, Christine (1997) *Greer: Untamed Shrew*. Sydney: Pan Macmillan Australia.

Ward, Elizabeth (1984) *Father-Daughter Rape*. London: The Women's Press.

Wilson, Elizabeth (1977) *Women and the Welfare State*. London: Tavistock Publications.

Working Grief (2015) <https://workinggrief.wordpress.com/>

World Health Organization (2002) *World Report on Violence and Health*. Geneva: World Health Organization, pp. 63–64.

Yousafzai, Malala (2017) <www.biography.com/people/malala-yousafzai-21362253>

Yousafzai, Malala <http://www.nobelprize.org/nobel_prizes/peace/laureates/2014/yousafzai-lecture.html>

BEYOND PSYCHOPPRESSION
Betty McLellan

A guide to therapy, which explores the intersection between the personal and the political. Betty McLellan surveys the development of psychotherapy and exposes the oppressive techniques of Freudian psychoanalysis, humanistic therapies, lesbian sex therapy and new age and popular therapies. She challenges the myths about women's mental and emotional illness.

… if you're interested in any form of psychotherapy or counselling as well as in feminism, then this is the book for you.

– Diana Currie,
Newsletter of Women with Disabilities Australia

ISBN 9781875559336

HELP! I'M LIVING WITH A ~~MAN~~ BOY
Betty McLellan

Translated into sixteen languages

What do you do when the towel is never picked up off the bathroom floor? How do you go about making men understand the difference between helping out with the housework and doing it? Have you ever walked through a supermarket with a thirty-five-year-old child who wants only the most expensive things on the shelves? And what about violence? Forty-one scenarios and solutions for the irresponsibility of many grown men.

Every woman will want to read it and every man should.

– Dale Spender

ISBN 9781876756628

If you would like to know more about Spinifex Press,
write to us for a free catalogue, visit our website
or email us for further information.

Spinifex Press
PO Box 105
Mission Beach QLD 4852
Australia

www.spinifexpress.com.au
women@spinifexpress.com.au